INTERNATIONAL INTERIORS

ARCHITECTURAL DIGEST PRESENTS

A SELECTION OF DISTINGUISHED INTERIOR DESIGN

FROM FOUR CONTINENTS

EDITED BY PAIGE RENSE

EDITOR-IN-CHIEF, ARCHITECTURAL DIGEST

THE KNAPP PRESS   PUBLISHERS   LOS ANGELES

DISTRIBUTED BY THE VIKING PRESS NEW YORK

Published in the United States of America in 1979
The Knapp Press
5900 Wilshire Boulevard, Los Angeles, California 90036
Copyright ©, 1979 by Knapp Communications Corporation
All rights reserved
First Edition

Distributed by The Viking Press
625 Madison Avenue, New York, New York 10022

Distributed simultaneously in Canada by
Penguin Books Canada Limited

Library of Congress Cataloging in Publication Data
Main entry under title: International interiors:
Architectural digest presents a selection of
distinguished interior designs from four continents
1. Interior decoration.   I. Rense, Paige.
II. Architectural digest.
NK2130.I54   747′.8′8   77-17004

ISBN 0-89535-003-3
Printed and bound in the United States of America

CONTENTS

FOREWORD

ARCHITECTURAL DIGEST INTERNATIONAL INTERIORS is a natural expression of our role as the international magazine of fine interior design.

In compiling this volume, we have had the whole world to choose from. The diversity and scope of this collection of homes from four continents confirm our belief that fine design—like fine living—has a worldwide unity in its many forms and variations. The means of expression may differ from place to place, but standards of design always bespeak imagination, self-knowledge and authority. Even as these varied homes in unfamiliar settings widen our frame of reference, I hope they also strike a familiar responsive chord.

In the United States, the examples of older worlds have contributed greatly to our sense of beauty and good living. I am sure that the significance goes deeper than the usual fascination with the exotic. In places where style has developed over many hundreds of years, the vagaries and changing fashions of the interior design field are put firmly into perspective. There is much to be learned from beauty that has shown its capacity to abide.

At *Architectural Digest,* trend is not a concept that has a great deal of meaning for us. That word usually describes a predetermined formula of things, colors and effects, as though following the right formula were the same as creating a satisfying interior design. Trends change from year to year and month to month, and who really laments their passing, after they have faded from the scene?

We prefer to speak of style, which is really a way of seeing and living creatively in the world. It is the ability to derive stimulation from almost any source, the capacity for excitement, the instinct for the best. It means not just the ability to choose the finest, but the creative spark to see how things fit together—to grasp vital connections that others miss. To have style does not mean developing a passive appreciation; it means projecting that appreciation joyfully and vigorously. The design of homes tests this quality in us: Just as painting and sculpture represent how we see, and music represents how we hear, interior design represents how we live.

At *Architectural Digest,* we have found that there are better ways of being journalists than filling our pages with lists of "things to do." We do not see the magic of fine design—style—as a series of techniques that can be duplicated. Rather, it is an approach to art and life that can be an inspiration. Concentrating on giving advice suggests that the creation of a magical home can be inspired from the outside. We believe it should come from within.

As reporters of fine international interior design, our role is to suggest ways of seeing, rather than to give advice. The varied kinds of homes we show speak of possibilities, not techniques. They show ways of being, in addition to ways of decorating.

The late Coco Chanel, whose own apartment was featured in *Architectural Digest,* once said, "Fashion passes, style remains." We do not believe that anyone has said it better.

We have chosen the homes in INTERNATIONAL INTERIORS to display this lasting quality of style. Beauty is here, from many ages and traditions. We might well turn our attention to these examples of beauty — not just to learn their lessons, but to absorb their spirit.

Paige Rense
Editor-in-Chief
Los Angeles, California

ARCHITECTURAL DIGEST   INTERNATIONAL INTERIORS

THE FLOWERING OF A LONDON FLAT

Michael Szell has a way with flowers. He cherishes them, photographs them, sketches them, collects them and prints them on the fabrics he designs. He covers walls, draperies, furniture and even the floor of his London living room with his own flower fabrics. Tabletops, too, bear an abundance of flowers, every one of them an orchid.

When asked to explain his single-mindedness, he answers in a candid and disarming way: "Orchids are chic." He has collected many of them on trips to the Far East and to South America. Indeed, for his next journey to the Amazon he has a permit that will allow him to bring back as many as twenty kilos of wild orchids. He takes care of them himself, and some he has had for ten years. The history and habits of each are familiar to him. They bloom twice in the winter, and then he sends them to a greenhouse in the country where they "sleep" through the European summer, which is really winter in their original environment. They are tough, but inflexible, travelers, and they never adapt to the seasons away from their natural setting. Each fall they are brought back to bloom again, and they appear at the popular Chelsea flower show, where Mr. Szell has his own stand.

The orchids, along with many other flowers, have naturally found their way onto the very special fabrics he designs. Michael Szell is willing to admit that in certain circles he is something of a household name. These circles are special indeed. The throne room at Windsor Castle, the J. Paul Getty Museum in Malibu, California, the Shah of Iran's palace in Tehran and British embassies around the world are decorated with his fabrics. For the great celebration at Persepolis in honor of the founding of the Persian Empire, tents were made from fabric of his design, printed with a bold Oriental motif. His fabrics, too, have been seen in such films as *Mary, Queen of Scots* and *The Great Gatsby.* To these ends he has spent many hours of research at the Victoria and Albert Museum and elsewhere.

For his own apartment, in a large Early Victorian house in London's Knightsbridge, he has deliberately created a different mood for each room. He wanted the bedroom dark for sleeping—warm and enveloping. But it does glow like a jewel box, largely because of the dark green printed linen on the walls, the color of malachite. The atmosphere, to be sure, is largely created by the fabrics, but there are many interesting pieces of furniture as well—among them, a handsome armoire, the only piece he managed to save from his family home in Budapest. Fortunately it could be taken apart, and it traveled well in a trunk. A number of the paintings are also family heirlooms and come from his grandmother's house in Vienna.

The entrance hall is resolutely cheerful and is surely a prelude to the feeling of the apartment as a whole. "It's very pleasant when I come home on a rainy night," says Mr. Szell. "After dark it's like a nightclub. The hall is my personal boîte."

Since he is such a great believer in nature, the drawing room clearly reflects his point of view. He makes extensive use of natural fibers, and everything is covered in white printed wool. On the floor is a large white Indian rug, and the problems of upkeep are considerable, though he is undaunted by them. "If I lose confidence occasionally," he says, "I never lack courage—or perhaps foolhardiness!" In the lovely large living room he has preserved the original Victorian details and proportions, but he divided what had been a smoking room behind it into the present bedroom, bath and hallway, with a dining room and kitchen beyond. In these smaller rooms Mr. Szell lowered the ceilings to maintain the proper proportions.

The large drawing room, however, does seem in many ways more appropriate to a house in the country than to a flat in London. Greenery appears everywhere to support the illusion. There is a green square in front of the house, and behind are the gardens of the Brompton Oratory. Michael Szell's drawing room blooms happily in the middle. The clear fresh fabrics in the room were inspired by his collection of Swansea botanical china. He is a patient collector, and it has taken him over twelve years to find some hundred pieces of it. It is fragile and most difficult to locate, since the factory only produced these particular faïence plates between 1790 and 1810. In addition, he has managed to gather together many of the original botanical prints that were copied for the pottery.

Michael Szell is reluctant to discuss his family and his aristocratic background. Growing up in Hungary, he left Eastern Europe after World War II. He attended the University of Aberystwyth, in Wales, and the Royal College of Art, and he studied for a year in Paris. He also studied with Sir Nicholas Sekers, who taught him the practicalities of fabric design. "He made me do all those things the very young, who are full of ideals, don't want to do," Mr. Szell says. "He used to ask such realistic questions as, 'Could you face that fabric with a hangover?'"

In general the designer credits his success in the field of design to hard work, and he considers that his background and his personal connections have had little to do with it. However, having grown up in a world of elegance and luxury, he is able to understand with considerable ease the requirements of an embassy or a palace. "That's something very lacking today," he observes. "Young people are inclined to be antagonistic to luxury, and so they have little conception of what is needed when the time comes to arrange a banquet or a ball—or especially to decorate a palace."

His own life is well regulated, and he is at his office early every morning. "Life," Mr. Szell points out, "needs a certain steadiness, I think. It's not really how bizarre or eccentric one is that matters."

What Michael Szell puts into life is a good deal of hard work, a generous measure of charm and plenty of good old-fashioned kindness. He helps his clients with finishing touches, even when his own responsibilities are long over. "You can't have a double life, you know," he says. "Being difficult in business and a nice person at home. Everything's part of a pattern, and I try to be kind."

Nothing gives Mr. Szell greater pleasure than giving a friend some simple and thoughtful gift: perhaps, for example, a basket filled with tiny cabbages and new French beans from his garden in the country. He is a very civilized man.

OPPOSITE: *In the Drawing Room, a gilt-framed painting by Bartholomew Dandridge occupies the center of an alcove. On the marble-topped table by William Kent, Brazilian orchids fill a Georgian ceramic bowl. Candelabra atop japanned tin vases from Pontypool, Wales, add glitter.*

RIGHT: *Fans of light rising from rows of English coach horns illuminate the Entrance Hall of designer Michael Szell's London apartment. Georgian mirrors with fluid tracery patterns are set against a brilliant silk wallcovering designed with panels of a repeated Persian medallion pattern. To heighten the drama of the entrance, Mr. Szell chose boldly patterned Bokhara rugs, with typically rich, vibrant colors. Lush green plants and orchids are evidence of the designer's interest in floral imagery.*

BELOW: *Eighteenth-century paintings—a portrait of the Duchess of Somerset by Sir Peter Lely and an allegory by Moroni of the Duke of York being led to victory—add a sense of solidity to the Drawing Room with its airy floral print. Above the Victorian fireplace is a regal tracery mirror that* formerly hung in Marlborough House. Queen of Siam Sirikite orchids bloom on the contemporary table. OPPOSITE: *A selection from Mr. Szell's collection of Swansea botanical china is displayed on the Drawing Room sideboard. The painting of three hunting dogs is by a pupil of George Stubbs.*

A VILLA OF
ELEGANT SIMPLICITY
AT NEUILLY

Neuilly-sur-Seine is separated from Paris only by the Bois de Boulogne, but the air itself seems different. To be sure, it is not exactly in the country, but there is the definite atmosphere of a small village. Streets, planted with chestnut trees and lined with high walls, rarely witness an automobile. From beyond the walls comes the fragrance of well-tended gardens. It is easy enough to imagine velvet lawns, clumps of rhododendrons in the spring, blue hortensias at summer's end and trimmed hedges behind which little girls play hide-and-seek under the eye of an English nanny.

Little by little, however, new apartment buildings have encircled these small islands of peace and greenery. For example, the exceedingly luxurious house where Arturo Lopez once gave the most magnificent parties in Paris has lost its surrounding park. And the Château of St. James, built at the time of Louis XVI, has kept its own park only because the building has been turned into a school.

Behind this lovely park is the house belonging to M. and Mme André Bettencourt. It stands on one of the most unchanged streets in Neuilly, well hidden by an iron fence and a screen of trees. The residence is nothing at all like the usual Parisian private house with its little courtyard and garden. Rather, it is a large villa, surrounded by tall trees and the sort of lawn popular at Deauville and Cannes some twenty years ago. The 1950s style is extremely rare in Paris, for in the years following World War II hardly anything at all was built, with the exception of apartment buildings.

The Bettencourt house, built in 1951 with classical symmetry, is reminiscent of a foreign embassy. There are enormous verandas, a long gallery serving as an entrance hall and a rotunda with rooms fanning out in every direction. On the right are a smoking room and a dining room; on the left, two formal salons. These wings do not continue in a straight line but veer off on an angle opening to the garden. The rotunda itself is the apex of the arrangement, while another circular area contains the vast sweep of the staircase with galleries on each side. On the walls of one of the galleries is a portrait by Girodet of Prince Murat, Napoleon's brother-in-law and chief of cavalry. It serves to underline the governmental aura of the villa.

M. Bettencourt is a statesman who has often been a government minister. He is also a well-known businessman. His wife is the daughter of M. Schneller, who founded one of the most extensive cosmetic empires in France. Mme Bettencourt is a tall, slim lady with reddish blonde hair, always impeccably dressed. The villa at Neuilly suits her admirably, since it is large, luminous and quite without unnecessary complications. Nothing, however, has been left to chance. Handsome bronzes are reflected on polished tables, and Khmer sculpture rests on pedestals. There are many impressive works of art in the house, but they do not suggest the static quality of a collection as such.

In addition, throughout the house a number of important paintings serve as striking accents. There is, for example, a large Le Nain dominating one of the salons off the rotunda—a canvas particularly appropriate to the area's massive proportions. Elsewhere there are paintings by Modigliani and Nicholas de Staël; a large canvas, Baroque in spirit, by Dufresne; and work by Pierre Bettencourt, brother of the owner. There is excellent sculpture as well. In the entrance hall stands a magnificent bronze by Maillol, portraying the figure of a young woman. There are also many examples by the famous sculptor of animals, Pompon, whose impressive grasp of simplicity complements the imposing sobriety of the décor in general.

A reluctance to use the elaborate, the bizarre or the involved is the hallmark of the two artists who have combined to produce the overall effect the owners wanted for their house. One of them, of course, they have never met: Emile-Jacques Ruhlmann, the great furniture designer of the 1920s and the 1930s. The other is Serge Royaux, whom many consider to be the most impeccable interior designer in Paris at present. That the talents of these two designers, so far removed from each other in time, have been successfully combined is primarily due to Mme Bettencourt and her father. In the 1930s

her father considered it inappropriate for a modern businessman to live in an imitative décor. He wished to be a man of his time, and he commissioned Ruhlmann to provide furniture for his house. Very soon they became good friends, rather than simply patron and master craftsman.

Ruhlmann himself worked in the tradition of the great cabinetmakers of the eighteenth century, using rare woods and a good deal of ivory. His scrupulous search for quality and his totally contemporary line—never Cubist nor merely functional—have made Ruhlmann furniture unquestionably à la mode, even today. Indeed, one of the finest examples of his unerring sense of style and proportion is the piano belonging to Mme Bettencourt. A piano is surely one of the most difficult pieces of all to reinterpret with any degree of originality. Ruhlmann, however, succeeded in producing a masterpiece of taste and technique, with a delicate balance maintained between practicality and aesthetic proportion.

When Mme Bettencourt decided to undertake some redecoration of her house, she sought the help of Serge Royaux, whose feeling for quality and whose disdain for the superfluous much appealed to her. He adapted his own style to the existing décor, and in the spirit of Ruhlmann he designed an enormous circular divan in the rotunda and a pair of low chairs covered in cut velvet. He added several Empire chairs whose formal and official style conforms to the general feeling of the Bettencourt villa. As is the case of any Royaux-designed interior, there are many vivid and lively accents: bright orange cushions and draperies, for example. M. Royaux, always respecting the architecture of the villa, nonetheless took it upon himself to cover the walls of the entrance hall and the galleries with stucco tiles made to look like travertine.

The décor he provided is architectural in feeling and eminently suitable for the residence of a statesman who entertains ambassadors and government officials regularly. Without being in the least somber, the house maintains the dignity that relies on pure quality and not passing fashions.

OPPOSITE: *Classical and modern elements fuse in the Rotunda of M. and Mme André Bettencourt's Neuilly-sur-Seine villa. A marble stairway with* moderne *tracery grillwork by Subes curves around a majestic Empire porphyry urn from the palace of Prince Murat.*

LEFT: *Glass doors open to the Entrance Hall, a long marble-floored gallery with walls of stucco paneling treated to resemble travertine. Only the gleaming form of a Maillol bronze, occupying a mirror-backed niche, punctuates the dignified, embassylike atmosphere.*

Blending grandeur and simplicity,
designer Serge Royaux shaped the décor
of the villa around a collection of
superbly crafted pieces by the eminent
furniture designer of the 1920s/1930s,
Emile-Jacques Ruhlmann. Several of
Ruhlmann's designs add distinction to
the smaller of two Living Rooms, a
light-hued, rounded room with
judiciously distributed dark accents.
LEFT: Highlights include Ruhlmann's
ivory-streaked ebony piano and a
17th-century painting by the French
artist Le Nain. BELOW LEFT: An Empire
bronze chandelier reinforces the shape of
the room, while raised vertical paneling
accents its height. RIGHT: Tall draperies
frame floor-to-ceiling windows and a
view of the large tranquil garden
behind the residence.

OPPOSITE: *In the larger Living Room, 16th-century Italian bronzes combine with Louis XVI and Empire furnishings to create an air of formality. A pair of leather-upholstered chairs by Jacob are grouped with a mahogany trictrac table. Draperies frame the entrance to an adjacent room.*

Walls covered in cut velvet provide a dense, warm background for art in the Study. RIGHT: An 8th-century Khmer torso combines grace and solidity in its simplified form. FAR RIGHT AND CENTER: Ruhlmann's rosewood chairs, a marble-topped table and urn-shaped lamps brighten a corner devoted to a collection of notable drawings.

RIGHT: Purity of design is perfected in the mirrored Dining Room. Marble in three colors creates a bold geometric floor pattern that contrasts with the quiet forms of Ruhlmann's amboyna furniture, Khmer statuary and a 17th-century Chinese celadon jardinière.

Built in 1951, when few private homes were being constructed in Paris, the stately villa relates stylistically to the 1930s. Very French in its symmetry and order, it has a solidity that is relieved by tall windows. The great expanse of immaculate lawn behind the house is a rarity—even for Neuilly.

TRADITIONAL IRISH CHARM IN COUNTY CLARE

Mr. and Mrs. Walter O'Connell of New York and Connecticut have been fortunate in fulfilling a dream shared by many another couple of Irish descent: to one day own a house in the lovely green fastness of Ireland itself. In County Clare they found a rambling manor house with stone barns and stables, and it seemed everything they had always dreamed about, an ideal place for holidays and a possible home for retirement. And both Mr. O'Connell, a horse breeder, and his daughter, an excellent horsewoman, were especially attracted by the opportunity to pursue their favorite sport in the scenic land of their ancestors.

The major problem, however, was that the handsome Irish manor house was in a sad state of neglect. Fortunately, Mr. and Mrs. O'Connell knew exactly what to do. They called on the advice of American interior designer Otto Zenke, who had done the décor for their home in Connecticut and was in the process of arranging the interiors for their New York apartment. When the designer arrived in southwestern Ireland to see the house for the first time, he saw what had to be done.

"Naturally, like the O'Connells, I wanted to restore it completely," he says, "and to bring back all its eighteenth-century graciousness. In the Victorian period someone had started to complicate the simplicity and elegance of the original house, and everything had gone from bad to worse."

Mr. Zenke's work as an interior designer is well-known, especially in the southern part of the United States; his main offices are in Greensboro, North Carolina. His activities, of course, have not been restricted to the South, and he has worked in other parts of the country and in Europe.

There were problems associated with the project in Ireland, however. There was not only the matter of distance, but there was the fact that the designer could not oversee the everyday work of a restoration that in the end took almost two years.

"When you can't be on the scene all the time," says Mr. Zenke, "it means that you have to plan very carefully. You can't afford to make mistakes, and that puts a great deal of pressure on any project.

But, for all the risk of failure, it was very exciting. I was determined to preserve a Gaelic feeling in all ten rooms of the house, to respect the traditions of the country and to make everything harmonize with the land. I think my insistence on these points gave a good deal of unity and cohesion to the end result. Ireland, of course, is a place of magnificent country homes and estates, and I quickly got into the mood of the countryside and the architecture.''

Along with Mr. and Mrs. O'Connell, he made careful studies of many other Irish manor houses in order to avoid any jarring notes that might destroy the harmony of the graceful eighteenth-century country life they wished to recreate.

"We did make some architectural changes,'' Mr. Zenke explains, "but they were minor. In the beginning what we did was simply clean things up a bit. Everything had become quite run-down. But there was much more work to be done on the interiors, and many of the changes were architectural in nature. Windows had to be made to reestablish the regularity of the eighteenth-century façade, new hardware and doors had to be installed, and, naturally, all the bathrooms had to be modernized. But the basics were really there from the start. It was just that certain things had been obscured over the years, and some charming effects had been lost. Take, for example, that glorious ten-foot window. It was there all the time, but someone had filled it in and put in a sort of powder room downstairs. We changed all that.''

The designer was in the enviable position of being able to select most of the furniture and accessories himself since the owners were not able to be in Ireland as often as they wished. "They didn't have anything specifically on hand for the house, in any case,'' he points out, "and they didn't really want to bring anything from the United States. So it turned out to be a field day for me, something of an interior designer's dream. Naturally, I relied on the owners as much as I could. They both have excellent taste, and Mrs. O'Connell in particular has a great sense of color and an excellent knowledge of furniture. Her husband, on the other hand, is more interested in paintings. We all agreed, of course, that the finished house would conform to its eighteenth-century origins, and there are very few contemporary pieces.''

Otto Zenke bought most of the antique furniture and objects in Dublin. He had been buying in Ireland for many years, and Dublin was a particularly convenient place, largely because all the antiques shops are in one area. He was also able, through his London office, to find additional pieces in England. Though the furnishings did come for the most part from Ireland, the designer had the upholstering done in England and brought the draperies from the United States. The latter were light and delicate, since neither he nor the owners wished to cover the windows totally, to obscure the magnificent views of the Irish countryside.

Throughout the two-story manor house as much use as possible is made of rich and cheerful colors: reds, greens and a good deal of yellow, Mrs. O'Connell's favorite color.

"Yellow certainly cheers up some of those bleak Irish days,'' says the designer. "And they definitely do have them, you know.''

Perhaps one of the loveliest parts of the completed house is the dining room, done almost entirely in shades of yellow. It is an important room for the O'Connells, who delight in entertaining. Indeed, all the rooms now function perfectly and seem at one with the Irish countryside. For the master bedroom in particular the designer made every effort to pay tribute to that countryside.

"There was a magnificent view through the windows of the trees and the barns,'' he says, "and there was no way I was able—or wanted—to compete with it. So, naturally, I didn't. I simply tried to continue the view into the room by using lots of green chintz and grassy green carpeting and a flowered pattern for the half-canopied beds.''

Otto Zenke will long remember his experience in Ireland and the opportunity he had to help an American family of Irish heritage contribute to the green land of their ancestors and to restore a certain measure of its antique grace and beauty.

The rolling hills of Ballingarry, stone barns and
stables, and a Georgian manor house lured Mr.
and Mrs. Walter O'Connell of New York and
Connecticut to establish a foothold in their
ancestral land. Designer Otto Zenke undertook the
complex task of transatlantic restoration.

A profusion of lily pads all but obscures the
reflection of the ten-room, two-story residence set
serenely among tall trees. Structurally typical of
Georgian manor houses, it attests to the
18th-century revival of interest in Palladian
architectural principles.

31

Shades of yellow infuse the interior with a cheerfulness that counteracts Ireland's frequently rainy days. BELOW LEFT: *Graceful windows remain undraped in the Entrance Hall, which is furnished—as is most of the house—with 18th-century Irish and English antiques.*

BELOW RIGHT AND LOWER LEFT: *In the Living Room, tall draperies and American upholstered pieces detailed in a bright floral print contrast with mellow antique wood furnishings.* LOWER RIGHT: *Italian landscape paintings echo the pastoral reality beyond the Dining Room window.*

Animal imagery pervades the Library, creating a congenial atmosphere for Mr. O'Connell, who breeds horses. A primitive hunting study dominates the room, and beneath it, on an antique pine mantel from Dublin, sit three Staffordshire dogs. A pheasant motif defines the upholstery of a comfortable wing-backed armchair pulled up to the glowing fireplace. Gimp trimming softens the corners of the room and the line of the dado molding.

BELOW: *A slightly elevated view from a window of the manor house looks out upon the nearby stables and smaller buildings of the estate. Rich green pastures provide both excellent grazing for horses and cattle, and a peaceful panorama of simplified natural beauty for human eyes.*

OPPOSITE: *An archway leads into a courtyard behind the main house where flowers and plants temper and add color to the aged, rough-hewn local stone architecture. Within this County Clare setting the O'Connell family captures a sense of life in an earlier, perhaps more harmonious, century.*

RIGHT: *A crisp flowered chintz lends quiet grace to a Guest Room and contrasts with the pristine whiteness of the coverlets and window trim. Fitting perfectly into a narrow space between the windows is an antique English dressing mirror.*

ROMAN COTTAGE

"Shall we talk about the French novelist Pierre Loti?" asks Rome interior designer Stefano Mantovani. The question is not quite so abrupt as it sounds, and the subject fits Signor Mantovani's mood and expresses well his own dramatic and original approach to design. The mention of Loti brings all sorts of delights before the eye: exotic reminiscences of a house on the Golden Horn; night scent arising from the gardens; moon-cast shadows of jasmine and lemon trees on chalk white walls; the luminous immensity of the great dome of the Eyüp mosque; bronzes; roses and turquoise silks— Constantinople of the 1890s.

"Now that's the sort of thing I like," says Stefano Mantovani. But why exactly Pierre Loti? Surely it is because this naval officer and novelist was one of the prime importers of Eastern magic for European consumption. Filtered through the Gallic viewpoint—ranging from the eyes of Eugène Delacroix and Gustave Moreau, to the shimmeringly cadenced prose of Pierre Louÿs and the valorous exoticism of Ravel—the trappings of the East graced the Belle Époque with a far surer mystique than that of the Turks themselves who crammed their palaces with Venetian and Bohemian glass.

In all events Stefano Mantovani is fascinated with Loti's *Phantom of the East* and his search into the opiate past for his lost love Aziyadé. He dotes on bright colors spread over black and silver—the essentials of Loti's image of Constantinople. Indeed, such imagery influences a good deal of the designer's work. Take, for example, an apartment he recently completed in Rome. Located on one of those winding lanes that cuts through the heart of the old city, it is an austerely Baroque building with the kind of monumental entrance that keeps the rest of the world outside.

One of Rome's most lionized young designers, Stefano Mantovani has always given his work an exotic flavor: an air of "silken dalliance," color excitement and pasha comfort. But perhaps nowhere else has he given these elements such freedom of expression as in this Roman flat he worked on with his associate Manuel Jimenez, who comes from Málaga, a city famed for having been Islam's last stronghold in Europe.

The result of their collaboration is an explosion of atmosphere and color that would have warmed the hungry heart of the Italian poet/patriot D'Annunzio, an exotic renowned for his eccentric and lavish tastes—both in women and décor. The style that designer Mantovani has chosen to employ is by no means inappropriate in the Roman capital. Arguably Constantinople was a Roman creation, and interiors with overtones of two former imperial capitals may be tantalizing for the historically minded. But perhaps that is not really the point. What does matter is the impact of the design, the *coup de théâtre* of this admirably selected collage. There are many elements at play: nostalgia for the Paris and London of the 1890s and a yearning for Araby with its heavily embroidered hangings that part in the imagination at the crash of a heavy gong.

Nothing could better express Stefano Mantovani's outlook. He has traveled almost everywhere, and now he wants his imagination to do the work—visualizing and recreating the scenes he has so often encountered. "Every time the curtain opens," he says, "there must be a new scene." And this is exactly what Roman sophisticates love. Left to their own devices, the Romans are perfectly happy to have their Baroque *palazzi* done up in the Baroque style and their contemporary houses done up in the contemporary style. But for all their seeming lack of imagination, they adore visual excitement when it is placed before them. And they have made the comforting discovery that Signor Mantovani can create a dream world that will be cozily livable and "quite right": stuff without nonsense. And it is not only the Romans. Curtains have been going up on Mantovani designs in Monte Carlo, Marbella, Geneva and Kitzbühel.

The apartment in the via della Lupa is old and small: two rooms, a bath and a kitchen. There is no terrace, no view and little light, since the narrow street keeps its seventeenth-century tightness until it suddenly comes to a stop in front of the magnificent façade of the Borghese Palace. There is still another reason for the spectacle and sumptuousness of the interior: Rome itself is locked out.

The entrance hall features two charming Gallé-designed vases executed in Paris during the 1890s, and they instantly introduce the Oriental theme of the living room. The accessories—and this is an essential part of the designer's art—come from everywhere. Not merely from the East, but East by way of the turn-of-the-century West, with Louÿs and Loti there to do the honors. The painting of a gorgeously appareled Nubian slave, dominating the room through its sheer size and glamour, is from London of the 1890s. There are also English watercolors of mosques and oases from the early nineteenth century, flanking a French oil that doubtless has a nodding acquaintance with Delacroix.

Above the voluminous divan hangs an elaborate late-nineteenth-century mirror from Naples. The bronzes, of the same period, are French, while the turquoise vases come from the courtyard of the Hermitage Hôtel in Monte Carlo. Another Oriental feature has been designed by Stefano Mantovani himself: The nest of tables in black laminated plastic and gilded wood is an elegant variation on a Japanese theme. From China come the elaborately gilded stools at either side of a pouf upholstered in an antique fabric from Afghanistan.

Perforated doors lead to the bedroom, and the walls are washed in chalky blue powder paint, called *azulejo,* "bluebird," by the Andalusian fishermen who use the color for their houses. The color itself forms a handsome background for the three great Medusa masks, Late Art Nouveau works that link the heyday of excess in Western design to the Oriental. It is amusing to learn that these stonily glaring heads come from an Italian cinema palace in the provinces from which they were ingloriously struck down when the grandiloquent in Italian design was vanquished by fluorescence and cement. The window is forgotten behind a sumptuous hanging of embroidered silk from Marrakech.

In every way Stefano Mantovani has designed an oasis for escapists—and taken the Golden Road to Samarkand with great style and panache.

OPPOSITE: *In the Living Room of his apartment on the via della Lupa in Rome, designer Stefano Mantovani evokes—with theatrical dash—the exotic spirit of French Romanticism. Views of Morocco, the colors of the harem and the glitter of brass accompany Signor Mantovani's designs.*

ABOVE: *Another view of the Living Room focuses on an ornamental openwork lantern from Morocco. As draperies, Signor Mantovani uses cotton banners from India painted with an overscaled lion and tiger—favorite subjects of the Romantic painters and poets. An elaborate 19th-century Neapolitan mirror graces a richly colored wall. In the foreground, a Philippine carved wood animal crouches atop a Chinese lacquered table.*

The Louis XVI daybed, large low pouf and contemporary Living Room sofa are laden with pillows covered in fabrics from India and Afghanistan. Mario Schifano's palm tree triptych enlivens a large portion of the far wall; above the Mantovani-designed bookcase is a painting of an enraptured Nubian poised against a patterned gold ground.

LANDMARK BEIRUT RESIDENCE

Overlooking both the Mediterranean and the Lebanon Mountains, the Beirut home known as *The Pink House* is remarkable, not only for its dramatic color, but for its relative antiquity. Dating from 1882, it is an uncommon vintage building for Beirut, a city fast becoming filled with skyscrapers.

The challenge of providing contemporary interiors for this venerable home was undertaken by one of the most innovative designers from the Middle East, Sami el Khazen, who has deeply involved himself in a flexible style he likes to describe as "Oriental contemporary." It is an intriguing blend of old and new, of East and West—with Islamic art perhaps the predominant influence. His interests and studies have carried him through many areas: painting, architecture, horticulture, couture. And these interests have combined to form the basis of a unique approach to interior design. For him good design is akin to good poetry—basically unchanging but open to different interpretations and different translations.

The Pink House is a clear illustration of his point of view. Originally conceived as a quiet retreat for work, the house was expanded to include living quarters as well as offices for design and architecture. The curves and geometric shapes of traditional Islamic interior architecture were used to create, in the designer's words, "a calm environment that evokes an atmosphere of tranquility."

The designer, who studied art in Paris and architecture in the United States, is a tireless worker who enjoys creating a project from the very beginning and achieving, both in the matter of interiors and exteriors, "a climate, an atmosphere, an organic unity." He uses whatever style or materials are necessary; and he ascribes this eclecticism to his Lebanese ancestors, world traders since ancient times and quite aware of international trends.

In this design, Sami el Khazen honored the traditional Lebanese penchant for a monumental living space by combining six small rooms of the old house. Nevertheless, he was careful to keep the scope of the area to human proportions by redividing it visually through the placement of sculpture and the variation of floor levels. The result is a large space separated into distinct areas that flow from one to the other without obvious interruption. Asymmetrically curved steps lead to the sitting area where most of the furniture is of his own design. Nearby there is a large arched doorway, whose overwhelming proportions have been scaled down by means of a crossbeam that disguises stereo speakers. The view through the arch extends to the sea across a spacious terrace that is a favorite place for relaxed summer entertaining.

Since the only natural light for the interiors comes from this open area, the designer has created a sophisticated lighting system with sliding panels used to control the sunlight. In an instant such flexibility can change the entire mood of any given area of this extremely large space.

"Lighting," says Sami el Khazen, "must have as many variations and possibilities as the changing moods of a beautiful woman."

The dining room, however, is one part of the large area with somewhat less maneuverability in the matter of lighting, since there is almost no natural light available. But the designer has created a solution by providing a glass-topped dining table with a dramatically illuminated fiberglass base. The area itself is the center of the progression of circles so characteristic of the central living space. The second tier of the floor provides seating, while the rise of the third, with its round foam cushions, serves as a backrest for the seating. Overhead, a moucharaby—through which harem wives in another era might have seen guests without having been seen themselves—supplies light and color. More light flows from a large adjustable arrangement of white plastic cylinders varying in height. The arrangement serves both to screen the dining area from the sitting area and to display, among other objects, a rare early Egyptian funerary jar.

Although he admires and uses fine antiques, he is inclined to display them sparingly. Perhaps the only exception is that part of the huge room devoted to music, where special lighting and mirrors set off permanent collections of Irish and Dutch cut crystal, Roman glass and Amorite pottery. It is a generous mixture of rarities that speaks of Sami el Khazen's familiarity, not only with European antiques shops from Paris to Dublin, but with the open-air souks of Cairo, Damascus and Beirut. A massive oak cabinet, in reality the only obvious divider in the large living area, houses a library and further collections of antiques.

One side of the dividing cabinet provides storage space for office materials and serves to define the working area. Focus here is on a large circular table of white painted wood with an aluminum base. Swivel drawers hold papers, and wooden shelves swing out to provide a place for those traditional ingredients of Middle Eastern hospitality—Turkish coffee and sweets.

Sami el Khazen's unusual approach to interior design, at once dramatically traditional and dramatically contemporary, has made him one of the most sought-after decorators in the world. Now based in Paris, he is continually traveling, completing assignments that take him from the coast of Spain to the great European capitals and to the oil sheikh-doms of the Persian Gulf. These international commissions are based to a large extent on his ability to design the appropriate setting for the people who seek his expertise, no matter where in the world they choose to live.

"The person who uses my services," he explains, borrowing terms from his background as an artist, "is an essential—perhaps the essential—part of my palette as a designer. He or she is always the most important ingredient."

However, as flexible and as conversant with various cultures as he is, the designer returns again and again to his central theme: "the contemporary interpretation of Islamic architecture." He describes with affection its lyricism, its symphony of triangles, its curves and undulations.

"For me it is very exciting to create something new in the spirit of the past," says Sami el Khazen. "That is where my intellectual satisfaction lies, and that is why I enjoy my work so much. For me it is certainly the best way to live."

For a Beirut residence known as The Pink House, *designer Sami el Khazen merged contemporary styles and traditional Islamic elements. In the Sitting Area, an architectural horizontal lowers the eyeline, and contoured platforms echo the shape of the arches.*

A sophisticated lighting system gently illuminates the arches leading from the sitting area to the Music Alcove in the foreground. Up-lighting brightens a collection of Irish and Dutch cut glass, while a Fatimid Dynasty sculptured niche appears golden against the pier in the background.

LEFT: *A shimmering sculpture-curtain sets off the Studio Area, which is further defined by an oak-paneled display and storage cabinet topped with a 19th-century Islamic cornice. In the background, the arrangement of cylindrical plastic modular elements and a colorful moucharaby bring proportion to the fifteen-foot-high vaulted ceiling.*

ABOVE: *Flowing levels—the highest, of laminated plastic—delineate spaces for working and entertaining. Cushions surround the Dining Area table, creating concentric patterns.*

On the large stone Terrace, the gnarled trunk of a wide-spreading shade tree emerges from a rustic stone-based table set for buffet; Persian designs inspired the hand-painted ceramic tile top. Sami el Khazen designed the stools and the geometrically arranged modular sofa platforms for sunworship and conversation beside the pool.

A GOTHIC RETREAT IN KENT

"Places are more important to me than possessions," says Christopher Gibbs. The philosophy of Mr. Gibbs, art and antiques dealer, is fulfilled with elegance at *Davington Priory*. It is a Gothic retreat amid swirling mists and yews, or a gentle outpost sustaining some corner forever England—depending upon the way you look at it.

Either way the present owner is well pleased with his Medieval ecclesiastical property—found, and bought by chance, some years ago as an alternative to life in London. During the course of the centuries it had been overlaid with successive restorations, but today all former embellishments have been pared away. The priory stands above the town of Faversham in Kent, an area of fruit growing and hop gardens within twenty-five miles of the white cliffs of Dover, where the Spanish Armada was first sighted. Below was a testing area where Royal Board of Ordnance gunpowder would topple a chapel tower with each explosion. Bridging the streams of Faversham Creek, past nesting swans and millstones dredged from the river, the squire of Davington Priory—striding ahead and looking most unmonkish in boots, apricot shirt and yellow cashmere—says: "Up there is my 'Jerusalem,' and down here the 'Satanic Mills.' Quite literally."

The priory was founded in the twelfth century and converted to secular purposes in the 1530s. Later on there were quite extensive restorations by Thomas Willement (1786–1871), a decorative painter and designer, and more work was done by the Church of England in the 1930s. Until as recently as thirty years ago Manorial Courts were held here, and much of the priory's character is due to Willement's abundant use of stained glass, most of which Mr. Gibbs has maintained.

Christopher Gibbs is very much influenced by William Morris and, although he owns nothing made by that famous craftsman, he surrounds himself with possessions of a kindred spirit: arts and crafts, pastoral Elizabethan décor and everything that is synonymous with a Falstaffian and perhaps mythical Merrie England.

In the entrance hall are fire dogs, a Field of

Cloth of Gold tapestry, a refectory table and candlelight—all creating the desired mood of antiquity. And pride of place is given to a painting depicting the Fool, a familiar character in Shakespearean plays. "He's a very important element in life," says Mr. Gibbs. "He is always with us."

The owner of Davington Priory walks toward the library, where a comfortable log fire blazes. The walls are covered in Lewis Day designs of green leaves. There are books galore, and tea is ready in gleaming white porcelain. At the point where the residence itself meets the church wall, Mr. Gibbs has rescaled a number of rooms with the collaboration of architect Nicholas Johnston. In such a way, a space with terra-cotta walls has been formed, and water cascades into a marble container. A shepherd's crook rests in one corner, and down a step there is a fragment from a Greek statue of the fifth century B.C., once used as ballast in the ship that carried the Lions of St. Mark's to Venice.

"I'd like to have gardeners bringing in tubs of camellias and many maids a-polishing," says Christopher Gibbs with a sigh. His attitude conforms to a most particular English idiom, as do the newly planted avenues of limes outside. The delight in surprises is also particularly English. For example, tucked away in lonely splendor behind the vegetable garden is a large cardinal's chair.

The upper floor of the house has myriad rooms, a number of them suggesting the sensuous influence of the East with their rugs and furs, their golden and mauve colors. A turretlike bedroom has Genoese velvet hangings and a handsome sixteenth-century bed from Warwick Castle. From here the owner, often clad in a shell-embroidered caftan and a nomad's yellow slippers, is the proud master of all he surveys.

"There's sturdy furniture here," he points out. "Shelves that don't collapse when you take out a book, chairs that can withstand all sorts of abuse. There is a certain robustness—the swing of a dog's tail would damage nothing. Perhaps I've arranged it all this way because Irish country life has always had a great appeal to me: the intense green of the landscape, the way things are done with handsome arrangements of furniture and the way in which the indoors and the outdoors are perfectly compatible.

"Surely," Mr. Gibbs continues, "the eighteenth century is not the be-all and end-all of architecture in this country. Personally I'm more interested in those special English interpretations of the philosophical and architectural ideas of an earlier era. Perhaps my interests are more scholarly. I'm not one for Chelsea porcelain, you know."

Certainly the atmosphere of Davington Priory is masculine, indeed a trifle deanish, and the hearty comfort and aura of antiquity would appeal to any Oxford or Cambridge don. "But I don't think a masculine look has to be drab and severe," Mr. Gibbs observes. "I relish beautiful stained-glass windows and lush Oriental rugs."

Even more interesting to the academic and the deanish is the fact that the priory is still filled with many half-veiled mysteries. Even though Mr. Gibbs, in his years as squire, has scraped away paint and uncovered at least six earlier layers, unearthing and uncovering many original fireplaces, there is much more to find. Layer upon layer of English history lies here for discovery.

Propped on a mantel is a copy of a 1915 photograph of the poet Rupert Brooke. Mr. Gibbs cheerfully admits, with a certain measure of vanity, that his own features resemble those of the famous poet. And the resemblance does seem rather more than a coincidence. There is something symbolic and mystical and very English about it. For in almost every way Davington Priory transmits a good deal of what one poem by Rupert Brooke defines as "furs to touch," "white plates and cups clean-gleaming," "grainy wood," "the good smell of old clothes," "the cool kindliness of sheets." There is a continuum here—near the imposing timber gates of the priory it is easy enough to conjure up the vision of a spectral dance before the dawn with a hundred vicars down the lawn.

The echoes of Rupert Brooke's lines are always present: "Stands the Church clock at ten to three?/And is there honey still for tea?"

Much of the Elizabethan character of gabled
Davington Priory *is a result of renovations made
by designer Thomas Willement, after he acquired it
in 1845. In his* Historical Sketch, *Willement
describes the materials that combine to form the
irregular checkerboard pattern of a lower wall, the*

*variety of window shapes, the wood carving of the
porch and other details of restoration. Colorful
strapwork-painted patterns recreate Medieval
architectural detail. The original Cloister Court,
surrounded by a low retaining wall topped with
guardian figures, is now a garden of
boxwood and old roses.*

An early-17th-century French gilded iron
chandelier, Oriental rugs and stained-glass
windows enrich the formerly monastic Entrance
Hall. Willement's designs for the tiles below the
fireplace were copied from the floor of the chapter
house at Westminster Abbey.

Not forsaking the Assembling of ourselves together, as the manner of some is: *Heb. 10.25*

An idea of the original 12th-century church decoration can be gained by examining the painted decoration and window design used in the Study. Coats of arms of various local religious houses ornament the walls near the painted ceiling beams. The interlace pattern of the window is punctuated by a heraldic emblem, and original 12th-century Caen stone curves around the doorway. Willement's 19th-century fireplace and finely painted and carved overmantel panel are framed by a trefoil Gothic arch. Furnishings include a 19th-century whatnot and a brightly upholstered window seat.

55

BELOW: *Sunlight streams through the unusually patterned bay window of the Master Bedroom. Antique fur rugs add warmth to the bare wood floor and modern platform bed. Accessories include a Chinese hardwood clothes rack and an 18th-century model of a plow.*

BELOW: *A Japanese gilt bronze lantern and a Grinling Gibbons mirror, both 17th century, complement the Library's 18th-century English furniture.* LOWER: *An upstairs Hallway, freshened with potted lilies, leads to 16th-century oak doors and a massive bed from Warwick Castle.*

This timeworn 14th-century stone curtain wall standing west of the priory is evidence of the historic origin of the complex. From 1153 until the 1530s the priory served as a house of the Benedictine Order, after which time the lease was sold by the Crown to a private individual.

VILLE MARIE DE MONTRÉAL

When a sometimes irresistible force meets a sometimes immovable object, the results are bound to be provocative. In the present instance the combination happens to be Jack and Tibby Leiby of Montreal. An interior designer formerly of New York, Mr. Leiby has a passion for antique furniture and period décor, African artifacts and chinoiserie. On the other hand, Mrs. Leiby, English by birth, dotes on her extensive collections of English porcelain and of contemporary art, which includes work by Calder and Vasarely. It is apparent that in their life together—and in their design outlook—certain compromises have been necessary.

For much of their married life Mr. and Mrs. Leiby, one of the couples most active in Montreal society, have lived in ten rooms of what many consider to be the most elegant apartment building in Quebec: *The Château.* It is an imposing fortress-like complex of baronial splendor, situated *centre ville* on Sherbrooke Street West. Montreal, of course, is a complex mixture of two distinct cultures and languages, French and English. It is, and has been, a city of turbulent change—politically, culturally and architecturally. It is a city where lovely rows of Georgian mansions have been razed to make way for supermarkets and parking lots, and much of the ancient architecture of Quebec has fallen to superhighways. But at the center of Ville Marie de Montréal—the city's original name—The Château happily remains an unalterable symbol of a bygone era of gracious living, an era firmly fixed in another dispensation. With its palatial dimensions, perhaps never to be duplicated, it is the sort of place where, as one Montreal writer has said, "you can comfortably relocate a whole household of furniture without putting half in storage."

It was here that Mr. and Mrs. Leiby decided to merge not only their lives but their remarkable collections of art and antiques and furnishings. To be frank, it was a difficult problem and its solution represents a fine example of marital and artistic cooperation. How was it all accomplished? "With diplomacy," says Mr. Leiby, and his wife raises a quizzical eyebrow. Her droll English humor and his more rapid New York manner blend well and offset each other most pleasantly.

"You have to remember," Jack Leiby continues, "that this is not the kind of apartment I would ever design for anyone else. This is very personal. We have joined our separate collections, and we have approached the mixture in a way that might not appeal to everyone. But we're the only ones who have to live here, aren't we?"

The Château apartment both satisfies their joint requirements as collectors and challenges Mr. Leiby's talents as an interior designer. The result is that their prized possessions are mingled without conflict. From the entrance hall, dominated by Ch'ien Lung pagodas and a Venetian Rococo console, to the dining room, with its collections of Mrs. Leiby's porcelains, to her husband's office, with its gigantic set of elephant tusks, its brushed-steel furniture and its gleam of lacquer—all is unified. The unity, it must be admitted, is a trifle grandiose and opulent. However, the mix of periods and styles is at once overwhelming and entirely appropriate.

Two living rooms, one a morning room and the other for formal entertaining, carry forward the rich mélange. In the morning room there is an impressive collection of Mason ironstone and a good deal of Rococo-style Chippendale furniture, along with a charming collection of papier-mâché snuff boxes. The more formal room, used for entertaining on a larger scale, is a further conglomeration of many different periods and styles. It is, in fact, the result of twenty-five years of collecting—and ten months of interior design work. Surprisingly, everything seems to blend with everything else, and perfect harmony reigns. Directoire candlesticks have been converted into lamps, and old and new are in constant juxtaposition. A white chair designed by Syrie Maugham nestles in one corner, while Louis XVI obelisks, African masks and a Vasarely construction merge into another arresting composition. Only the disciplined hand of an experienced interior designer such as Jack Leiby could have kept it all from looking like a disorganized fantasy.

The dining room is rather more the domain of Mrs. Leiby, and it is far less dramatic than the formal living room, yet quite as highly styled in a simpler and perhaps more subtle way. Essentially it is the stage for her extensive collections of china, and in order to offset these collections in the most effective way possible Jack Leiby chose one of his favorite colors, a soft and unobtrusive damson plum. Here again the old meets the new, and there is no apparent conflict. A modern table, lacquered in a plum tone, rests on a carpet designed by David Hicks. But there are many antique objects: Adam candelabra, an 1820s Spode dinner service, mid-eighteenth-century stemware and Irish silver, a delicate Hepplewhite console. Tibby Leiby's porcelain collections are everywhere.

Quite as dramatic as the living room, but with an entirely different atmosphere, is the bedroom. It resembles a warm fabric tent and basically gives the impression of being a nest. It has something of the flavor of a romantic 1930s room of the imagination—a room where one might expect to find Garbo lounging enigmatically on the brushed-steel four-poster bed. A cheerful black and yellow geometric pattern carpets the room, and the painted ceiling is enlivened by a surprising and delightful floral border. Scattered here and there around the room is Mrs. Leiby's new collection of coquillage, an interest she proposes to pursue professionally: "I seem to have evolved from silk flower arrangements to putting shells together in geometric forms."

Mrs. Leiby has a newly acquired interest in shells, but her husband adheres to his old passions—particularly in the matter of collecting chinoiserie. Would it be possible for them to reach some common ground of interest?

"Well, of course," says Jack Leiby with a laugh. "We both love Eskimo art, and that's what we are concentrating on at the moment."

Even a hasty glance around would seem to confirm the fact that there is little more room in the apartment for anything else of any style or period. But fortunately the apartments in The Château are large and generous—quite as large and generous as the many interests of Jack and Tibby Leiby.

An aura of dark mystery pervades the Entrance Hall of Mr. and Mrs. Jack Leiby's Montreal apartment in The Château. *Set like jewels against a backdrop of bronze mirror, Louis XVI chinoiserie figures, Ch'ien Lung pagodas and a George II barometer glow in the light of a Georgian lantern.*

The eclectic result of twenty-five years of intensive collecting, the formal Living Room is organized around a central axis consisting of an elaborate Venetian garden chandelier and, atop a draped octagonal table, a contemporary sculpture of Belgian black marble. Lacquered walls and ceiling, a boldly patterned fabric used for draperies, shades and sofa upholstery, and a Ch'ien Lung twelve-panel screen create the setting for a profusion of objects that includes collections of African sculpture, chinoiserie and contemporary graphics.

Architectural details, such as a satin-lined niche, accent the stylized Dining Room where Tibby Leiby displays her antique porcelain collection. Mid-18th-century English stemware and Irish silver complement the 1820s Spode dinner service.

BELOW: *The traditional bed canopy effect is extended here to completely encompass the Master Bedroom. Trimmed with the same English chintz that covers the brushed-steel bed and edges the ceiling, the calico wall draperies tie back to reveal mirrors, vitrines and doorways.*

ABOVE RIGHT: *A collection of Coalbrookdale and Derby porcelain and elaborate shell arrangements by Mrs. Leiby grace the polished surface of an Empire bureau plat in the Master Bedroom.*

PRIMITIVE SOPHISTICATION ON THE COSTA DE CAREYES

Architect Marco Aldaco, a Yaqui Indian from northern Mexico, builds houses in a manner many would consider primitive—with results that are nothing less than spectacular. He builds without specified plans and has only contempt for standard architectural procedures.

Unorthodox, perhaps, but this intense independence has brought to Marco Aldaco such people as Aristotle and Jacqueline Onassis, Gloria Guinness and Antenor Patiño. And for Gian Franco Brignone he built this enchanting house on the Pacific coast of Mexico. It is the pacesetter for other villas that will be spread thinly over seven miles of rugged coastline at Costa de Careyes.

"The error of today's architects is that they work in offices with T-squares," says Marco Aldaco. "They might as well be working in factories. They plan houses as if they were making the same Ford car over and over again.

"Architecture, for me, is not an industry. I don't draw plans. I don't have a T-square or a ruler. I do everything with my feet and my hands and my head. I suppose I am like a sculptor who makes a sketch of what he wants to do. But he doesn't hand the sketch to some workman and say, 'Make this statue.' No! I make a thousand sketches for a house, but I do *not* make plans. When we begin to build, I take off my shirt and get my hands dirty and work right along with my men."

Gian Franco Brignone, an international banker and real estate developer, wanted to provide Señor Aldaco with a detailed topographical plan of the site, lying between Manzanillo and Puerto Vallarta. The idea seemed reasonable enough.

"I didn't want it," the architect relates. "I told him, 'I'm not in some office in New York. I am here. With my feet I will walk and measure the land.'"

For Marco Aldaco such is the beginning of the creation of a house as *una obra de arte,* and he describes the process with enthusiasm.

"I go alone to the land," he explains. "I don't want anyone with me. I cannot build a preconceived house, and I must understand the land. I take off my shirt and feel the sun and walk all over the property. I feel the cold at night; I feel how the winds blow; I spend time with the land. I sit and walk and eat on the land. I go again and again.

"I see how the sun moves and the birds fly. I think about the history of the place and the people. In this case the owner told me there were a certain number of square meters of land for the house—but he had not seen the stars at night. I spent time there, and I saw the stars and the distant islands and, far away, a lighthouse. And I thought: The house must see this lighthouse. So I decided to put a window in the bedroom that would frame it."

Only after studying the land, the view, the climate, the history—the "entire cosmos of the place"—does Señor Aldaco begin to consider the specific needs of the owner.

"Such problems are easily handled," says the architect. "The important thing is the house itself." But he is also quick to add: "The personality of the owner is very important. I am particular about my owners. I need someone who can help me—through his personality—build a great house. He is my collaborator." Frankly, however, the ideal owner in Marco Aldaco's opinion lists brief requirements and then collaborates with the architect by leaving him completely alone to wrestle with the creation.

"There's a long period when I don't know exactly what I'm going to do," he says. "I suffer a lot. I don't sleep. I am in a bad humor. I fight with all my friends. I don't speak. I am angry, because I cannot make the house come to life. I feel useless, and I am sad. Then one day, while shaving or playing golf or driving my car, I have the intuition, the inspiration. I give birth. It's almost as if I were a computer. I feed the computer all this information about the land and the people, the area and its history, the owner and his specific needs. Then at last the computer says, '*This*, Marco.' And on that day I call my friends and apologize for the way I've behaved, and I promise we'll drink champagne because a new house is born."

Then he sketches his inspiration, working furiously to capture ideas before they escape. He makes hundreds of quick drawings—not plans.

"Then I go back to the land again with my little drawings and bags of lime," he elaborates. "I draw the house on the ground itself with lines of lime. The land tells me where I have made errors."

With no plans on paper, how does he proceed? "I mark with a stick the place where a wall will be. I say to my workmen, 'Look, this window is going to be as wide as your outspread arms and half the height of your body.' They understand."

Completed, the Brignone house is a precise statement of Marco Aldaco's architectural philosophy. "Fundamentally I consider architecture as space expressed," the architect points out. "The space in this particular house is continuous. Everything is curved. The space doesn't know where it begins and ends, and that is magnificent. I think corners in a house are knife blades. They are offensive and serve no purpose. Houses only have corners and right angles because architects draw plans with *T*-squares and rulers.

"Use curves instead. They help people think. You know, a person is more tranquil in an environment of curves. Man's entire body is curved, and he developed in the curve of the womb. The spirit must be fed, and my houses are for people.

"Consider the extraordinary view from this house: the near and distant islands, the water breaking over rocks, the inlets from the sea, the entire Costa de Careyes in every direction. But let me tell you that it wasn't as beautiful when I first saw it. It was not as beautiful, because there was no house. It was simply a view without limits. Now the view has even more grandeur, for I have put it in frames. Every window, every opening in the house, is a frame for some particular part of the view.

"People cannot understand everything at once," continues Marco Aldaco. "We see and comprehend in parts. With walls and windows I have emphasized the views—and at the same time reduced them in scope so that they can be understood. The panorama is the same, equally wonderful, except that people are now able to *see* it."

And Gian Franco Brignone, who has only one eye, with happy accuracy named the house *Mi Ojo.*

LEFT: *The land and its history guided architect Marco Aldaco when he designed* Mi Ojo, *a residence of visual poetry on Mexico's Costa de Careyes. "The space in this house is continuous," he says. "Everything is curved. It is a house for the spirit; the spirit must be fed."*

ABOVE: *Perched on a sheer cliff of a promontory extending into the Pacific, the house basks in sunlight and tranquility. All windows face the exhilarating vista of rugged coastline, deep blue water, gentle inlets, near and distant islands, and luxuriant tropical vegetation.*

Open to the cooling breezes, the living room, dining area and kitchen are sheltered by a conical palapa thatched with palm leaves. Coconut palm trunks, each entwined by a rubber plant, provide support so flexible that the structure is capable of withstanding either earthquake or cyclone.

BELOW: *To preserve the uninterrupted flow of space, almost all the furniture was built into the Living Room, and a bed of pebbles was geometrically inlaid to resemble a rug. The Dining Area, pierced by the palm and rubber plant columns, is a shaded loft above the living room.*

LEFT: *With a panoramic view of the Pacific and the intricate structure of the* palapa *to enthrall the senses, the prosceniumlike Dining Area requires minimal decoration. Traditional Mexican chairs and pillows that restate the hue of sea and sky satisfy the demands of comfort.*

BELOW AND BELOW RIGHT: *All exterior and interior walls of the Bedroom Wing were handfashioned without molds; surrounding cacti, low palms and* fuego de primavera *flourish. A native vase marks the characteristically curved stairway to the wing.*

70

A gentle counterpoint of verticals and horizontals creates subtle architectural strength in the Master Bedroom. Set into a niche in the floor, a triangular sofa provides a commodious vantage point for contemplating the ocean view framed by a tall window open to the wind and sea air.

OPPOSITE: *In a Guest Room, the bed floats on an architectural platform bordered by rustic pine shelves. A tapestry provides a colorful focal point, and Jalisco artist Jorge Wilmot's stylized ceramics inject a playful note.* RIGHT: *A window in a Guest Bath captures a turbulent view of waves dashing against the rocks. Señor Aldaco maintains that a view has more grandeur when framed: "Every window, every opening in the house, is a frame for some particular part of the view."*

RIGHT: *Bamboo lattice supported by small palms and rubber plants shelters the rooftop terrace from an abundance of sunshine.* FAR RIGHT: *A rough-textured, earth-toned wall rises like a pre-Columbian monument above the tropical paradise of the Costa de Careyes.*

A PARISIAN ANTIQUAIRE'S LEFT BANK HOME

Jean Pierre Hagnauer is one of the leading antiques dealers in Paris. He is actively involved with the biennial Salon des Antiquaires and the even more prestigious exhibition that is held each May in the venerable Hôtel George V, where the best shops show their best merchandise.

Even in this distinguished company M. Hagnauer's display stands out, for he always dazzles the eye with something charming and picturesque. His favorite era—and the one in which he has become a specialist—is the end of the eighteenth century, the period from Louis XVI to Directoire. His collections include magnificent chests signed by Leleu and Oeben, chairs that are at once grand and comfortable by Jacob and innumerable tables gleaming softly in bronze and mahogany. All of this furniture, once fought over during auction sales at Christie's and the Hôtel Drouot in Paris, rests peacefully now in his antiques gallery, which has the delightfully intimate aura of a private home.

The shop, which adjoins the apartment, has no display window and is known only to important collectors and sophisticated amateurs. It is on the rue de Seine, not far from the Institut de France in the heart of the art dealers' district of Paris. To reach the shop the visitor passes through a porte cochère dating from the early eighteenth century. The building is at the end of a small private courtyard, a little below street level, and there is a charming garden on the other side. The house originally belonged to Mme Hagnauer's grandfather, a distinguished surgeon and brother of the art critic Élie Faure. And here, in the middle of the nineteenth century, Rosa Bonheur, celebrated painter of animals, also had her studio.

The Hagnauer apartment looks out over a narrow garden that is always green, variously planted with bamboo, rhododendron and azalea. Beyond the bushes are a number of ancient houses and a wide expanse of sky. The *jardin d'hiver* and an enclosed balcony give this side of the house a Victorian flavor, and Rosa Bonheur's enormous studio has become the salon.

Jean Pierre Hagnauer seems more like some

courtly amateur collector of the last century than a present-day antiquaire. Everything about him is understated, reassuring. He says little and is content to let his remarkable collection of furniture make its own statement. He started his career as a businessman, but in 1945 he became an antiques dealer and interior designer. He was largely responsible for bringing back into fashion English mahogany and the simplest examples of Louis XVI. But he also created a new interest in the elaborate patterned rugs of the Second Empire, as well as Chinese cachepots and Indian fabrics. His teacher was the famous Georges Geoffroy, a decorator of the most exacting taste, whose influence can be seen extensively in M. Hagnauer's present apartment.

At the beginning of his career Jean Pierre Hagnauer worked for many well-known people. Jean Cocteau asked him to arrange the décor of his country house near Fontainebleau, and the actor Jean Marais had him design the interiors of a houseboat. Over the years, however, M. Hagnauer grew more and more interested in antiques, and gradually they came to dominate his life and his career. Now he is satisfied simply to give clients good advice, and he no longer troubles to oversee the various annoying mechanics of decoration. On occasion he does design modern furniture, although such work is rarely found in his shop. His own thoughts on décor are well worth considering:

One: Above everything else, respect the thrust of the architecture. Do not decorate a vintage 1930s apartment in a Louis XV manner nor make a Pop statement in some Louis XIII château.

Two: Reject those trends of the moment that force interior designers to accept objects of poor quality under the guise that they are "amusing."

Three: Reject any literal and painstaking re-creation of historical periods. In the long run such an approach can only be static and boring.

These suggested rules are very much in evidence in the apartment he and his wife share. Jacqueline Hagnauer runs her household superbly and also takes time out to watch over the shop when her husband has to attend an important sale in London or Geneva. The only difference between the shop and her salon is that the shop contains more sumptuous furniture and fewer paintings.

These paintings, mostly from the nineteenth century, add great panache to the salon and call to mind the era in which this wing of the house was built. For many years M. Hagnauer has been collecting the minor masters of the final quarter of the nineteenth century, painters who adroitly captured the essence of the Parisian scene: its theaters, racetracks, cafés and salons. Some of the artists are very like the Impressionists, Degas in particular, and others paint with that minute attention to detail so characteristic of the early Dutch painters. Still others worked in a Symbolist manner. Each of these artists had a more or less special area of interest: Bérard, the world of the demimonde; Louise Abbéma, the world of young actresses; and Clairin seemed to concentrate exclusively on portraits of Sarah Bernhardt. In their day these painters earned enormous sums of money, exhibited regularly at the Salons and worked in studios done in the style of the Hagnauer salon, now happily simplified.

But the large salon does retain many of those elements so dear to nineteenth-century studio painters: an abundance of green plants in cachepots, flowered Victorian rugs, Chinese cloisonné vases and urns brought to France during the Second Empire, Louis XVI chests, elaborately tufted and upholstered furniture. Over the mantel is a particularly important canvas, a nineteenth-century still life in the Japanese manner by Louise Abbéma. At first glance the salon may seem very crowded indeed, but the sure hand of the designer is over all.

Seen from the dining room in the half-light of evening, the enormous room takes on a theatrical quality. Through large windows the fading Paris sky, always more mauve than black, looks like a giant stencil beyond the trees. It is a setting that would be appropriate to a Henry James heroine—calm, elegant, filled with undefined allusions and significant silences. Is it necessary to point out that Jean Pierre Hagnauer has not seen fit to change the décor of his apartment for many years?

LEFT: *One of two modern steel-and-glass tables beside the sofa in the Salon holds objects relating to the earth, and a finely worked 18th-century Chinese cloisonné lamp.*
FOLLOWING PAGES: *The large, light-filled Salon—once the studio of Rosa Bonheur—retains its 19th-century flavor. M. Hagnauer achieved the effect with an abundance of green plants, a flowered Victorian rug and a mixture of soft upholstered furnishings and Louis XVI antiques. Displayed on an antique easel are paintings by Boudin, Bérard, Bonvin and the Comtesse de Noailles. Russian screens in ebony and ormolu soften the corners of the room. A painting by Louise Abbéma, done in the Japanese manner, hangs above the Louis XV marble chimneypiece adorned with 18th-century candelabra and cloisonné bottles.*

OPPOSITE: *An unusual 18th-century armchair designed by Georges Jacob in the Chinese taste stands near the luxuriant draperies that demarcate the Salon from the adjacent fabric-upholstered Dining Room. A pair of Russian chairs attends a fine Riesener game table.*

ABOVE: *Eighteenth-century chairs surround a crisply draped dining table; the Russian chandelier, pineapple-shaped bronze candelabrum and candlesticks on the painted console fill the Dining Room with soft light. The bookcase by Leleu came from the château at Saint-Cloud.*

83

OPPOSITE: *An assemblage of equestrian paintings, both antique and modern, enhances a wall of the warm-toned Study. Classically inspired ormolu candlesticks placed at either end of the marble mantel flank M. Hagnauer's intriguing collection of small wooden boxes that resemble traveling cases.*

BELOW: *Vine-patterned walls provide the Master Bedroom with a vital backdrop for antique furnishings. Elements in rich mahogany—a cylinder desk, the chair beside it signed by Jacob and the unusual 19th-century settee—contrast with the pristine clarity of the canopy bed.*

MOROCCAN ARABESQUE

High on a cliff above the beach of Tangier, York Castle has dominated the Strait of Gibraltar for more than four hundred years. The fortress has seen many a conqueror come and go; it has been occupied by the Portuguese and the English, by Moorish sultans and Barbary pirates; it resounds with the mystery of North Africa and the splendors of the Gates of Hercules. Dating from the sixteenth century, the crenellated fortress was built by the Portuguese when they first occupied the old Moorish city. It fell into English hands in 1662 on the occasion of the marriage of Portuguese princess Catherine of Braganza to Charles II of England. As part of a generous dowry, the lady brought with her the city of Tangier. Curious about his new possession, the English king sent an artist to make engravings of the city and its fortress. Today these engravings hang on the walls of York Castle.

The name of the castle is not quite so inappropriate as it appears to be, since it honors the Duke of York, brother of Charles II and governor of Tangier during the English occupation. The day came, however, when the Moors drove the English from the city, and in their flight the retreating forces paused to bombard the fortress. It was rebuilt by the Moorish commander, and, as the years passed and new invaders came, the castle was put to many different uses, some of them ignominious indeed— as stable and storehouse, as garrison for the sultan's Black Guards, as prison for the victims of the Barbary pirates. By the twentieth century, it was totally abandoned and almost entirely in ruins.

It took a Frenchman of great flair and imagination to have seen the possibilities of this awesome relic. He is a Parisian of surpassing taste: Yves Vidal, former president of Knoll International. M. Vidal was struck, as so many others have been, by the unparalleled setting of York Castle and the exotic appeal of Tangier. He was not content to regard the castle simply as a picturesque ruin, however, and he soon began to imagine it as a magnificent and unusual holiday retreat for himself. Rising near the casbah of Tangier, the fortress lies in a setting of high romance. All the evocative cities of Morocco are close at hand: Fez, Rabat, Marrakech, Casablanca. M. Vidal could resist no longer. He acquired the majestic ruin and set about the challenging task of rebuilding it—not only to serve his own requirements but to reaffirm the ancient glories of the fortress. The result is far more than a replica. York Castle has been brought into the contemporary world with a flourish, at the same time retaining all the mysteries of its most forbidding and grandiloquent past.

The extensive restoration not only required the talents of Yves Vidal himself, but also the help of interior designer Charles Sevigny, an American living in Paris, and Robert Gerofi, a Belgian architect living in Tangier. Together the trio made a careful study of local architecture and the history of the castle. They were aided immeasurably by the engravings commissioned by Charles II.

While the building created by owner, architect and interior designer is almost entirely new, all the traditional architecture of the past has been scrupulously duplicated. Roofs and walls were restored to their original state, columns replaced and the ruined interiors brought back to life. In almost every instance, the architectural detailing of the ancient fortress was followed. Other traditional aspects of North African architecture were as carefully duplicated, often copied from neighboring buildings. There are whitewashed walls, the undulating curves of doorways and arches and windows, the terra-cotta red ceilings and the green doors regularly seen in Morocco. There is an octagonal court open to the sky and totally surrounded by arcades. In the center of the court is a swimming pool surfaced with tiles made at Fez; they are exact reproductions of seventeenth-century models. In the same way the interiors maintain a fidelity of setting, many of the walls having been covered with local moucharaby screening, often backed with silk. And Yves Vidal made a point of emphasizing wherever it was possible, both in the interiors and the exteriors, that traditional and particularly restful Moorish combination of water and green plants and brightly colored tiles.

Scrupulous as the exterior restoration has been, the new interiors of York Castle strike a somewhat different note. To be sure, the Moorish atmosphere and the elements of Islamic architecture are present, but they have been subtly redefined. In fact, while retaining a North African flavor, the interior décor makes use of a great deal of contemporary European and American furniture. At the same time the décor is characterized by a rich and eclectic assemblage of furniture and objects from almost every part of the world and from almost every period of history. Both the simplicity of the contemporary, however, and the richness of the traditional conform to the thrust of Moorish design, itself a paradoxical mixture of clean lines and dazzling arabesques.

As created by Yves Vidal and Charles Sevigny, the interiors contain a dramatic mixture of elements: some Moorish, some European, some new, some old. It is true that the initial impact is one of extreme simplicity. There is strikingly contemporary furniture by Eero Saarinen, Florence Knoll and Harry Bertoia. But a closer look reveals the many ornate objects that M. Vidal has collected in every part of the world: Thai silk cushions, eighteenth-century mirrors of great complexity, Cambodian Buddhas, Siamese pillows, nineteenth-century Persian flasks, Moroccan rugs.

York Castle is large. However, the basic lines of its architecture are simple; thus there is no feeling of excessive décor. Rather, there is an overwhelming sense of space and tranquility. Despite the many Baroque objects and dazzling fabrics the redesigned fortress contains, the mood is one of starkness and quiet—exactly, it must be added, the mood Yves Vidal wished to create. Today the fortress, astride the great cliff, is quite as commanding as it has ever been. But now there is nothing ominous about it. York Castle is no longer a fortress or a prison or a garrison. More happily, it is a bold and elegant tribute to past and present, a rare combination of Europe and North Africa. And, it can safely be said, there is nothing quite like it anywhere else in the world.

OPPOSITE: *Stationed at the edge of a sheer cliff above the beach at Tangier, one of* York Castle's *ancient battlements commands a view across the Strait of Gibraltar to the coast of Spain. Built in the 16th century, the strategically positioned fortress once played an important part in North Africa's history and for centuries guarded the city.*

LEFT: *Major restoration began after M. Yves Vidal, shown here in native attire, acquired the picturesque ruins of the castle.*

LEFT: *Open to the sky, and at the heart of the castle, is an octagonal Court surrounded by Moorish arches and Fez tiles. Repeated patterns of arches and reflections of pierced and glazed Moroccan lanterns are visible both day and night in the placid rectilinear pool, an addition that cools the setting. M. Vidal, together with interior designer Charles Sevigny and architect Robert Gerofi, studied local architecture and the history of York Castle in order to breathe new life into the majestic structure; the roof and walls were restored, terraces added and a new interior created.*

FOLLOWING PAGES: *At the top of a tower, the Moorish-shaped windows of the Master Bedroom frame a sun-drenched view of Tangier and the entire bay. The contours of the arches and the crenelations of the open turret cause a rhythmic recurrence of architectural shapes.*

The updated design of the Dining Room exemplifies calm, symmetrical simplicity. A Moroccan lantern is centered between pointed arches fitted with a tracery of moucharaby and softened by potted plants. Saarinen chairs and dining table merge monochromatically with the rug.

A 17th-century pikeman adds a whimsical touch to the whitewashed wall at the end of one of the long arcades bordering the central court. A Guest Room, its bed covered and canopied in a rich woven tapestry, opens onto the arched vista and applauds the approach to elegance through simplicity.

ROMANTIC GRACE FOR ENGLISH CITY AND COUNTRY LIVING

Open the front door of the London house of Diana Phipps and forget the rigors of the English climate. The red paisley fabric on the walls gives an immediate feeling of warmth, and meeting Mrs. Phipps is an excellent tonic, too. Her houses—one in London, one in Oxfordshire—represent an overwhelming amount of her own hard work; yet neither her energy nor her sense of humor ever flags.

She decorates her houses on impulse and would willingly do nothing else. Much of the work involved she does with her own hands. She can make almost anything, reassembling bits of this and that to new glory, and her virtuoso feats with a staple gun are little short of miraculous.

"I never throw anything out," she says, "and I always reuse what I have. If I started from scratch—buying whatever I liked—I would feel cheated. I decorate like an emigré!"

An emigré of a special kind, it must be added. For her early childhood was spent in luxury on the Continent, and her family divided their time between three castles, one of which they had owned for eight hundred years. Her father was Count Leopold Sternberg, and her mother had been the Countess Cecilia Reventlow-Criminil before her marriage. When everything was confiscated, the family huddled in a flat in Prague, where they lived for the last three years of World War II. Their houses and lands were returned to them in 1945, but by 1948 everything was taken again—this time never to be returned. And so it evolves that the present decorating talents of Diana Phipps spring from a quick wit and a quick hand. In any case, possessions seem to mean little to her.

She came to London after the death of her American husband, Henry Phipps, and she now divides her time between a Victorian house in Notting Hill and a Queen Anne parsonage near the Thames in Oxfordshire. Both houses reflect her creativity and hard work. And, in addition, the country house reflects the artistic talents of her mother. The Countess Sternberg has painted a number of murals for the Queen Anne parsonage, and her purpose seems to have been quite as practical as it was decorative. Portraits of all the flowers that bloom in the garden have been painted on the entrance hall paneling, for example, to conceal cracks caused by the central heating, and a fresh green and white mural in the bath conceals some disliked gray fixtures and walls. Her daughter also paints: charming watercolor sketches of houses and interiors. Mrs. Phipps binds these together with magazine clippings of rooms she likes; occasionally she adds the clipping of a room she cannot stand, just to keep her from making the same mistake.

There do not seem to be many mistakes, however, in the two houses she has arranged for herself and for her mother. A keen eye has served her well, and in the London house she has added a number of stunning architectural details that greatly enhance its charm: doors and frames, paneling, balustrades and moldings. Most of these were salvaged from nearby houses about to be demolished or found by searching assiduously through junk shops all over London. "The Portobello Road and the Bermondsey Market are unbeatable," she says of her constant forays in search of objects and accessories. "They are, I think, still the best in the world."

The entrance hall of her London house is usually cluttered with faded treasures awaiting paint, gilt, staples or glue. If there is some work she cannot do herself, she will find a craftsman who can. Cast-iron candlesticks have been gilded; an incomplete wrought-iron bamboo balustrade, copied and made whole; and a garden pergola, created from commonplace materials. Above everything else, she prefers to do whatever work is required herself. She has covered all the walls and many of the ceilings with fabric. Draperies, upholstery, cushions, billowing swags above the bed—she has made them all. No detail is too small, no extra work too much. She repaints statues if the color is not exactly right, edges bookcases with gilded picture frames, covers shutters with velvet and puts a decorative border on all her shelves.

Her magpie tactics proceed more with enthusiasm than with any particular concern for finding rare antiques. Once, she remembers, she bought a fragment of a painting in the Portobello Road: "I wanted something long, red, narrow and cheap; and there it was." Friends raised their eyebrows, until the fragment was authenticated as part of a larger work by Rubens that had been destroyed.

Her energy seems inexhaustible, and there is no amount of work she will not do. "For the living room in the country," she explains, "I originally hung the Javanese batik just as it was printed, in long oval patterns. Then I thought: I can't have all those pies and cakes on the wall. So I took the fabric down and repieced it. I was very bad tempered for a week." But now the ovals have been reduced to make circles, or elongated to make arches—both far happier solutions aesthetically.

The final result of all this hard work and careful attention to detail is that both her house in London and her house in the country are marvelously comfortable and relaxing. And surely Diana Phipps does deserve the occasional moment of respite. Perhaps her favorite place to relax is in her country house, restful and tranquil in exactly the way a country house should be. There are naturally some personal and unusual touches. There is, for example, a swimming pool built into the barn; the barn doors slide open onto a daffodil meadow sloping down to the Thames.

Decorating for Diana Phipps is a pleasure, and she is always ready for more. She has done two houses in London, one in the country, along with the conversion of a barn—and she always has time to help her friends. "But when they ask me to decorate professionally," she says, "I don't dare. All that business about payment would be too difficult. And strangers never ask."

They ought to; they would have a tremendously good time. Diana Phipps, searching through London's shops in silk shirt and blue jeans, discovers with a keen eye and an attitude free of the mundane. In her mind decorating with delight and romance takes precedence over rules and traditions. The result: houses done with spirit, where every room holds some lovely surprise.

ABOVE: *On a London street with a row of Early Victorian dwellings, the pastel façade of this four-story townhouse at once strikes the eye. Diana Phipps has never depended on wealth for her sense of style: She is a wizard at improvisation and resourcefulness, and each room of her house attests to her ingenuity.*

ABOVE: *A plush suede-wrapped mattress/sofa provides a cozy spot in the Living Room.* ABOVE RIGHT: *A church railing, a raised platform and draperies enclose an intimate tented area of the Living Room that is accented with an exotic painted bust.*

OPPOSITE: *Dark velvet-covered walls unify the double Living Room. Slender gilded columns at once divide the two areas yet keep them open. The majority of furnishings are arranged in a 19th-century manner. The imposing portrait in the foreground is by Sir Henry Raeburn.*

LEFT: *Mrs. Phipps created a countrified look in the Kitchen. All the wall surfaces, paneling and appliances have been given an antique finish.*
BELOW: *The Dining Room is an airy and open gardenlike space. Carved chairs and a table from India and an Indian print fabric used in the alcove area combine with the wrought-iron staircase and Victorian ceiling to create an exotic effect. A painting by James Reeve hangs on the denim-covered wall above a Georgian table and tureen.* OPPOSITE: *An inventive gathering of gingham creates an inviting Guest Room.*

OPPOSITE: *Now a peaceful retreat in Oxfordshire along the banks of the Thames, Diana Phipps's Queen Anne country house, built in 1703, had been used as a parsonage for 250 years.* LEFT: *Garden flowers painted by Mrs. Phipps's mother, Countess Sternberg, are set into the Entrance Hall paneling. The French papier-mâché clock above the fireplace has mother-of-pearl inlay, and a Derby ginger jar graces the Georgian side table.* BELOW: *Mrs. Phipps recut and repatterned the Javanese batik wallcovering to fit the Living Room architecture. Casual denim and batik are used for the upholstery, while refined Italian Louis XV chairs complement a Louis XVI trictrac table.*

A warming fire increases the pleasures of bathing. Fanciful wall paintings by Countess Sternberg, a French chandelier and accessories that include an antique towel rack, a tiered stand and a delicate wicker chair give this Bath the pleasing effect of a civilized sitting room or boudoir.

BELOW: *Mrs. Phipps's Bedroom is graced by a baldachin and bedcovering made of a lively flower print. Pillows are covered with old Spanish lace, quilting and a Provençal print.* BELOW RIGHT: *A sculpted bust of a woman irreverently sports a flower-trimmed straw bonnet.*

ART AND HISTORY IN THE GREEK COUNTRYSIDE

At the pull of a rope a monastery bell clangs and, moments later, a small door in the massive gate swings open. Historic *Pyrgi* is revealed: its garden of dazzling colors, the wild profusion of herbs and flowers and blooming shrubs, a complex of three low buildings and two towers. The complex itself is arranged agreeably around three small courtyards.

The owner is Ian Vorres, an urbane and amiable Athenian who, together with architect M. Photiadis, has created this charmingly rustic retreat. In an atmosphere laden with history Ian Vorres, the biographer of the Grand Duchess Olga of Russia, can work peacefully and without interruption.

"At the moment," he says, "I'm writing a life of Alcibiades, the controversial Athenian general and playboy who came to fame during the Peloponnesian War. Actually, he was born near here."

Situated in the hills of ancient Attica, remote—but not too remote—from Athens, the house provides the writer with everything he needs. Not only is it ideal for work and entertaining and relaxation, but it provides an authentic setting for his vast collections of Greek art and antiquities. Yet why would an author, who has lived abroad for many years and has seen much of the sophisticated world, choose this relatively isolated and rustic setting?

"In 1964," he explains, "I came back to Athens from Canada where I had lived for some fifteen years. Frankly, I was appalled at what I found in Greece. My countrymen were in the process of destroying one of the most beautiful environments in the world by building houses made of cement blocks, houses with no character at all. They seemed determined to eliminate all traces of Greek character and tradition. I owned a flat in Athens, but I felt the best thing for me to do would be to find something outside the city, something historic that I could expand and restore and return to its original beauty. Luckily I found it here in Paiania. At the beginning what I had was no more than a cluster of three houses and a stable. But they had been built when Greece was under Turkish domination, and the echoes of history were here."

A careful man, Ian Vorres did not plunge into

the project of restoration until he had made a considerable study of the area and of other houses in the immediate neighborhood. "Before making any changes at all," he points out, "I took perhaps a thousand photographs of buildings in the surrounding countryside. After this I was able to devise a plan that would tie all the units of the small complex together. The property itself is quite large, and the problem of expansion and addition offered no obstacles," he explains. "I made a point of relying entirely on local artisans and of using indigenous materials. Exterior walls, as you can see, are built of local stone, and we used the dry construction method—without mortar. It is a dying art that only the oldest artisans understand. The rest of the walls are made of stucco and are whitewashed in the traditional Aegean style."

Although insistent on following all the time-tested methods and recreating the atmosphere of an ancient land, he nevertheless managed to provide the perfect contemporary setting for himself.

The interior has been arranged to afford as much room as possible, and rounded arches indicate room divisions effectively without actually hampering the feeling of space. And more rounded arches carry the theme forward by framing the windows. There are smooth stone floors, rough-textured white walls, handhewn ceiling beams and handwoven rugs and draperies.

"Although I'm a biographer and an art critic, as well as a newspaperman and a businessman," says Ian Vorres, "I really think I'm primarily a collector. With me collecting is something of a mania, I will admit. And I was fortunate, too, in inheriting a number of very interesting pieces. The *laica*—those objects one can find in even the humblest house—I have collected myself over the years. These are things like wellheads, mortars, horse troughs, the millstones in the garden. I pick such things up wherever I find them. For example, I made a dressing table out of a baker's bread bin, and I treasure an old barber's chair with a back that slides out. You'll notice that all the dining room furniture is made from antique doors I collected in Ma-

cedonia. A piece of wild oak I'd bought to make a door was so beautiful that I used it for a table top—and the rest followed.

"When I first came here and started buying up everything the villagers were throwing away," he continues, "they started to call me 'the crazy American.' But I'm certainly not American, and I don't think I'm crazy. After a while the villagers began to see the point, and they don't seem in such a hurry now to pull things down and throw them away. So perhaps I've accomplished something."

His collections, however, include far more than millstones and Macedonian doors. There are innumerable interesting objects from the past: among much else, an eighteenth-century church reredos from northern Greece, a fanlight of the same period from the Cyclades, amphorae dating from the fifth century B.C. He is particularly proud of a collection of decorative plates, which covers more than half of one wall in the large reception room. They depict events in the lives of Greek royalty, along with mythological scenes.

"I've had these plates for about six years," he says, "but I very much doubt if you could even find one today. I'm also a keen collector of ancient Greek coins, and I think I have one of the most comprehensive private collections around. But perhaps my most valuable possessions are three pairs of carved and gilded icons made of wood. They are called *vimothirai*, and they are doors from the inner sanctum of a Greek Orthodox church. And probably the most ancient object I have is an ax head from Thessaly. It's from the Bronze Age."

Eventually it is his intention to leave Pyrgi and its contents to the village of Paiania as an ethnological museum and a repository of Greek history. The idea has created a considerable amount of interest in the village, and crowds of people have been arriving at the main gate seeking admittance.

"I've told the gardener to turn them away as gently and politely as possible," says the owner of Pyrgi with a gracious and patient smile. "He is to say that Mr. Vorres is alive and well, but that *after* he dies they will be most welcome."

OPPOSITE: *In the town of Paiania outside of Athens, biographer/art critic Ian Vorres shaped historic* Pyrgi. *Linking together and restoring several village buildings dating from the Turkish occupation, he established an authentic setting for his extensive collection of Greek art and antiquities.* RIGHT: *In the Living Room, a rounded arch bisecting a pitched ceiling, clerestory windows, rough-textured walls and a smooth stone floor create an active architectural context for traditional Greek artifacts and indigenous textiles, rugs and furnishings.* BELOW RIGHT: *A courtyard abloom with flowers complements walls whitewashed in the age-old Aegean manner.*

Medieval oak doors from Macedonia became the table, chairs and benches in the Dining Area. Underscoring the room's center beam is a portion of Mr. Vorres's extensive collection of decorative plates portraying Greek royalty, historical figures and mythological subjects.

An arched doorway leading from the dining area into a large reception room can be closed off by a studded wooden door that slides along a lintellike beam. As in the exterior architecture, rough cornerstones project from the rendered wall, illuminated by a clerestory window overhead. Further examples from Mr. Vorres's antique plate collection and a flotilla of old ship paintings bedeck the wall in orderly array, while a carved stone corbel and crude stone pieces appear to be placed at random for a contrastingly spontaneous effect.

OPPOSITE: *In the Reception Room, dark wood furniture of local manufacture merges with paintings, pierced demilune windows and iron candleholders to infuse the atmosphere with Byzantine echoes. Softening the feeling are classical amphorae and sculpture.*

RIGHT: *Jewellike in color and ornately framed, an 18th-century reredos from Northern Greece adds solemn brilliance to a stark whitewashed wall. Slender iron candleholders are linear accents amid solid wooden forms and a massive stone jar sprouting a bouquet of dried flowers.*

*A vertical column of 18th-century Cycladic marble
demilune windows, surmounting a Thessalonian
Star of David, accentuates the height of the Tower
Study—a transformed stable. Beneath the
overhanging sleeping loft, icons glow golden against
stone walls inset with antefixa.*

In a Guest Room, nestled between the lantern-lit sleeping niche and the rustic pitched-wood ceiling, an oblong panel with delicate fretwork cuts into the textured masonry. A beam above a window serves both as a valance and as a shelf for displaying decorative objects.

HONG KONG PENTHOUSE

Although his origins are quintessentially American, there is little doubt that interior designer J. J. Killough III is indeed a citizen of the world. His many travels and the fact that he has lived for long periods in such metropolitan centers as London and New York would seem to confirm it. That he decorated an apartment for himself in the mysteriously exotic setting of Hong Kong leaves no doubt at all about his international status.

"My family was in business and in ranching in Texas," he explains. "But I wanted something rather different. At first it was my idea to be a sculptor. Then someone told me that architecture was the highest form of sculpture, and I studied architecture at the University of Texas. After serving as an officer in the navy, I began working in New York for Edward Durrell Stone. Eventually I thought it would be a good idea to start off on my own. But first I took a trip around the world and fell in love with Hong Kong."

His Asian penthouse apartment was designed to display a dramatic view of the famous harbor. Light pouring in from every direction prompted Mr. Killough to call his penthouse a "cottage in the sky," because its resulting freedom and sense of space are delightful features he could never find in similar apartments in London or New York.

"My doors are always open," he says, "and my friends seem to find my home a pleasant gathering place. People come in droves—often they are uninvited! No matter. Ordinarily I give about five small or intimate dinner parties a week. I really prefer to entertain no more than six people at a time. I did have a big round marble table in the penthouse dining room, but it wasn't very congenial. So I eliminated the dining room, thus providing the latitude to serve dinner anyplace in the apartment."

The unorthodox and the unusual, it must be said, are the hallmarks of J. J. Killough's approach both to interior décor and to life itself. There are many sides to his personality—and even certain confusions about his exact profession. He regards himself as having four separate professions: architecture, interior designing, furniture manufacturing and real-estate development. His thoughts are, inevitably, outspoken and unconventional. And although he is presently based in Houston, Texas, this multifaceted world traveler feels that "the home of my heart" is in London.

Surely rules and the opinions of others have never guided either his personal life or his professional career. Its flavor definitely Oriental, his Hong Kong apartment merely confirms the fact that he believes in a generous mixture of all styles and all periods. In fact, he has gone beyond the concept of eclecticism into a realm where even that word is not sufficiently descriptive. The apartment became a rare cornucopia. In one surrealistic gesture an antique French chair hangs from the ceiling, replacing a chandelier. And the rooms overflow with Oriental furnishings and art Mr. Killough acquired from such unusually exotic places as a Buddhist monastery in Macao and a seventeenth-century church in the Philippines. Ming temple garniture blends with eighteenth-century English furniture and a Chinese opium bed. Yet the people for whom he designs seem very happy to accept his approach and his rather autocratic methods.

"I must have carte blanche," he says. "No one should expect to move in tomorrow. Interior design is an emotional thing for me—a feeling more than anything else. I don't sit down and plan everything ahead of time. Many people fight life, and they end up by not doing anything at all. So I try to let things evolve—but, if at all possible, on my own terms! As you can see by the Hong Kong penthouse, I have the disease of collecting. My family were all collectors, so I come by it naturally. Even when I was sixteen, I was drawn to Chinese porcelain, and I remember persuading my mother to buy a pair of Sung Dynasty vases. I've gone on from there. I think that all my clients become avid collectors, as well. Maybe because I'm a little forceful with them. But don't misunderstand—possessions aren't the important things in life; people are."

In a curious way, despite his international life and the fact that he has lived in one of the most exotic and evocative cities in the world, the designer feels that his experiences have made him more American than ever. He found Hong Kong a strange and rewarding society in which to live. Out of almost eight million people, there are perhaps forty or fifty thousand Europeans and Americans, and they are divided in every way imaginable, with their own customs and social lives: Britons, Spaniards, Americans, Belgians, the Dutch—and so forth. At the beginning Mr. Killough remembers that "it was almost necessary to have a passport to go to a dinner party." It took over a year for him to become accepted as more than a transient.

"Living abroad in a somewhat isolated and detached position," he explains, "made many things much clearer to me. I began to think about things I had never really thought about before. I thought about our own politics and customs and economics, and somehow things took on a different perspective. In terms of my particular interests, I came to understand the principles of architecture and interior design more realistically. At first I was critical of American design, but then I became very proud of it. I saw things far more clearly than I had in London or New York."

No matter where he lives, he carries with him the treasures he has accumulated over the years along with the understanding of design with which his cosmopolitan life has rewarded him.

"I live with antiques," says J. J. Killough, "but I feel that in the area of design I'm somewhere in the twenty-first century. I don't mean that to sound as if I think I am ahead of anyone else. It's simply that I've lived in so many different places and have traveled so much that I think I have some feeling for the future. And the future has to produce—politically and emotionally and aesthetically—some form of international cooperation. There has to be a Common Market of the spirit. That's the only way political problems can be resolved. It's definitely the only way people in my profession can benefit from the experience of others and learn to appreciate all forms of design. I love them all, and I've collected as much of everything as I was able. Too much, perhaps—but still not enough for me!"

Atop Victoria Peak, the Hong Kong penthouse designed by J. J. Killough III—a "cottage in the sky"—faces the harbor, Kowloon and mainland China. The interiors reflect the evolution of Mr. Killough's extensive collection of Oriental art and furnishings. OPPOSITE: The Entrance Gallery previews the treasure-filled apartment. Vertical accents—an arrangement of 18th-century watercolors of Chinese tradesmen—produce a heightening effect. Architectural features were added to display objets d'art: an antique Philippine leather breastplate, South African coral and a miniature bronze cannon from Macao occupy a niche. The Greco-Roman chair supports a whimsical porcelain cat, and a Ch'ing blanc de chine vase serves as an umbrella stand. RIGHT: Buddhist temple hangings and fragments of antique Chinese screens surround the entrance to an informal Sitting Room. Beyond, a Peking glass lantern illuminates antique Chinese porcelains and a low banquette laden with pillows.

OPPOSITE: *A ceramic ram poses proudly at the entrance to the Study. Mr. Killough's desk, an antique Chinese altar table, stands before a twelve-panel coromandel screen. The large Sung urn is filled with a dramatic overscale arrangement of palm grass and rolls of architectural drawings.*

ABOVE: *A portrait from the school of George Chinnery—the British painter who introduced oil on canvas to the Orient—is asymmetrically placed above the mantel in the Living Room. Serene 17th- to 18th-century Spanish santos stand on the parquet floor and on a shelf. To the right of the door is a glass-encased figure from Ming Dynasty mythology—one of the eight Taoist immortals.*

Sparkling harbor lights and the mainland hills can be seen above the grillwork of a sheltered terrace adjoining the Living Room; the aged horse near the terrace steps is a Ch'ing copy of a T'ang sculpture. Eclectic appointments include antique English, French and Chinese furniture.

A contemplative Kuan-Yin from a Buddhist monastery, a famille noire vase and other Oriental porcelains rest on an elaborate painted and lacquered antique Chinese table. Mounted on the wall behind the table, amid prints and watercolors, is a collection of gold and silver betel nut boxes.

OPPOSITE: *The Bedroom is complete with an "opium bed" made from 18th-century pierced carvings. A brilliantly glazed Ch'ing vase tops a stack of painted and lacquered wedding chests beside the bed.*

ABOVE: *On the Terrace, a sunburst made from mid-19th-century English wrought-iron transom grilles is suspended above a table set for an intimate dinner. A Wan Li water jar in the foreground and bird cages containing porcelain figures enrich the evening ambience.* RIGHT: *A Philippine bronze lantaka points toward the teeming Hong Kong harbor.*

A
SECLUDED ROMAN
VILLA

It is amazing, but true, that there exists in the heart of Rome, quite hidden from view and completely removed from the perpetual snarl and roar of motor traffic, an exquisite jewel box of an eighteenth-century villa surrounded by gardens and a park. No less amazing is the fact that the villa was created in 1925 and that the tremendously tall conifers—cypresses, Lebanese cedar, Korean and umbrella pine—were planted at the same time.

It came about that Prince Philip of Hesse and his bride, Princess Mafalda of Savoy, discovered in a detached corner of the *Villa Savoia,* then situated on the outskirts of Rome, a little *casale* that was to become the nucleus of the villa as it is today. They transformed what was no more than a tiny house, enlarging it to its present dimensions and naming it *Villa Polissena* after a mutual ancestress. In the eighteenth century the Princess Polissena of Hesse had married King Charles Emmanuel IV of Sardinia, who died in 1735. Thus even then the branches of the family trees of the Houses of Hesse and Savoy were intertwined.

The villa became the home of Prince Philip and his wife and remained so until the death of Princess Mafalda in 1944. Today their second son, Prince Henry of Hesse—a painter who also designs opera sets, an amateur gardener and a man of great taste—shares the villa with his father, Prince Philip.

Its charm is many faceted, based to a large extent on the fine proportions of the house itself, the sensitive treatment afforded each architectural detail and the harmonious relationship between the villa and its surroundings. To an impressive degree both villa and gardens are the result of intense personal involvement on the part of the owners.

"My wife planted these trees from cones," says Prince Philip, pointing to the spreading tops of two umbrella pines, now at least fifty feet high. His late wife also planted the large cypresses, now a semicircle of tall dark spears in back of the formal garden. Naturally Prince Philip himself has always continued his interest in the gardens. He points with pride to a dwarf Japanese maple: "It was brought from Japan in 1910 or 1912, I think, for the first Roman production of *Madama Butterfly*. When the opera closed, someone gave the tree to a gardener, and it ended up here."

There are many other trees to occupy his attention as well. In the Japanese garden, for example, is a small grove of bamboo trees with an unexplained gap in the middle.

"Oddly enough, the bamboos shift around on their own," explains Prince Henry. "Their roots move underground in some mysterious fashion, but this hardly bothers my father. He has always felt that at the end of every vista there should be some man-made object—like the head of Hercules on top of that tall column. So the gap in the bamboos is ideal, and one day we'll put something there."

Among the many exotic trees surrounding the villa is one of unknown origin that in the fall produces a small number of delectable fruits similar to limes in appearance but of quite different texture. Oddly they combine the flavors of strawberry and banana. Also in the fall wild, edible mushrooms spring up on the lawns. They are gathered and cooked and eaten with great relish.

A double row of cypresses that leads to the villa from the main gate ends abruptly, and deep shadows give way to bright sunlight. Here, framed in the formal parterres centered by a pool from which a majestic seventeenth-century Triton on horseback emerges, stands the house itself. Roman orange in color, accented in glistening white marble and set against a whole gamut of green, it seems to glow with pride in its own perfection.

In contrast to the luxurious gardens the entrance hall of the house is rather severe. Each of the three reception rooms opening from it has been given a distinctive character. The grand salon is mainly Italian, although no attempt has been made to create a period piece. The dominant features are three large eighteenth-century wall panels sculptured in high relief. There are other delights as well: a large niche containing a collection of blue and white Ming porcelain, a ravishing marble mantel attributed to Giovanni Piranesi and a floor paved in marble fragments from the ruins at Ostia Antica.

Of the two smaller salons, one has the lightness and gaiety of chinoiserie, the walls covered with Ch'ien Lung painted paper scenes. The third salon, whose walls are hung with large eighteenth-century Japanese panels, has as its most important work a portrait of two young men by Van Dyke. Despite a certain formality, however, all three salons are charming and inviting—and entirely comfortable. There is nothing pretentious about them.

But surely of all the rooms in the villa the most personal is Prince Philip's study. Situated on the third floor and opening onto a terrace, it is where the prince receives his intimate friends. It is quite informal and cozy, the walls papered in a medallion pattern and closely hung with the prince's collection of drawings, including work by Callot, Piazzetta and Van de Velde. One wall is given over to books, and there is a vitrine filled with small and precious objects, many of them by Fabergé. Satin draperies and a crystal chandelier add sparkle to the room, and it is a happy room, full of memories and full of present endeavors. Here the prince is at home with his family, his special friends and his remembrances of the past. That past stretches back through generations, and there are many present reminders of European royalty of another century. On one table, for example, stands a pivoting portrait medallion on one side of which is a bas-relief head of Queen Victoria and on the other a bas-relief head of Prince Albert. They were, in fact, the great-grandparents of Prince Philip of Hesse.

A remarkable sense of the continuity of history is felt in this charming villa. Not only is the history of Rome itself suggested on every side, but there is the larger continuity of the vanished world of nineteenth-century Europe—with its traditions, its aura of grace and privilege, its passionate belief in the future. Quite another world now lies beyond the towering cypresses and cedars of the villa, and there is little doubt that the spirit is refreshed by the graceful journey into the past offered by the Villa Polissena. There is nothing forbidding about it, nothing ostentatiously regal, perhaps only a wistful feeling of loss and of gratitude.

OPPOSITE: Villa Polissena, *the Rome residence of Prince Philip of Hesse, exudes an aura of antiquity that belies its 1925 creation. Rising from a placid pool in the formal garden, a 17th-century sculpture of Triton and his mount contributes to the classically inspired ambience.* LEFT: *Moss-covered steps ascend a gentle hillock in the park surrounding the villa.* BELOW LEFT: *Ivy envelops a bust of the youthful god Hermes.*

A statue of Jupiter and another of a female nude punctuate an axis of the formal garden, illustrating a concept Prince Philip supports: Every natural vista should terminate with a man-made object. From this view, the perspective culminates in a glimpse of the vividly painted villa.

BELOW: *A view from one of the villa's upper terraces reveals the symmetrical design of the formal garden and the prevalence of topiary shrubs and classical statuary. A patterned inlay of rocks adds detail to the pavement and repeats the geometry of the parterres.*

FOLLOWING PAGES: *The classical mode continues in the Grand Salon, which is dominated by the architecture: high-relief wall panels, painted ceiling panels and a floor paved with marble fragments from Ostia Antica. Ming porcelains add a crisp note to the mellow atmosphere.*

Hepplewhite chairs and a mahogany table contribute an English aspect to the formal Dining Room. A marble dado and wall moldings enrich pastel-toned walls; the bold carpeting reinterprets marble. A Neo-Classical-style frieze circles the room, complementing 18th-century drawings.

OPPOSITE: *In the Chinese Salon, alive with fantasy, chinoiserie-painted wallpaper panels evoke the Ch'ien Lung period while the airy papered ceiling creates an illusion of birds in a bamboo cage.*
BELOW: *A view past the Chinese and Grand salons to the garden juxtaposes diverse cultures.*

ABOVE: *Art of the world's great cultures—a Chinese goddess in the grand salon and Triton in the garden beyond—enriches the villa and makes it a repository of history.*

CHEZ HENRI SAMUEL

The more popular a designer becomes, the more prestigious his following will be and the more he runs the risk of giving in to the conventional. Letting himself be influenced by the beautiful furniture he sees in the houses of the wealthy, he could easily fall prey to an ultrarefined taste that could become unimaginative.

For many years now Henri Samuel has understood how to maintain his position as one of the leading decorators in Europe without being forced into any conventional mold. He has always kept up the interest in new trends that has consistently marked his career. He has not become associated with any one style in particular, unless perhaps with what might be called *le style Rothschild*. No doubt this is because some twenty years ago he decorated Baron Guy de Rothschild's château at Ferrières. He also arranged a residence for Baron Edmond and designed the interiors for Baron Alain's mansion on the avenue Marigny in Paris.

Le style Rothschild, to which Henri Samuel has given a new life, is remarkably eclectic. It shares this characteristic with many another impulse evolving from the Second Empire. Flourishing in the middle years of the nineteenth century, that style took its inspiration from a number of different periods and cultures. These ranged from the Renaissance to the reign of Louis XVI, from the Orient to the world of Ancient Greece and Rome. Damasks, velvets and tapestries dominate the style, and the designer often feels it necessary to add a stark accent—a Giacometti sculpture, for example.

When the Shah of Iran's sister asked Henri Samuel to decorate her apartment in Paris, he placed her Eastern antiques in an Art Déco setting. But when Gérald Van der Kemp asked him to help arrange the First Empire salons at Versailles, he kept scrupulously to the décor of the period. The same care and attention to detail was apparent when he decorated portions of the Grand Trianon in the park of Versailles. Closely following sketches by artists who had worked at court, he reproduced antique draperies and reupholstered furniture from the former palace. Today one of the finest illustrations of his taste can be seen in the Metropolitan Museum of Art in New York. Mr. and Mrs. Charles B. Wrightsman donated four splendid rooms to the museum, and they insisted that Henri Samuel take part in the arrangement of the French furniture.

M. Samuel has created many magnificent interiors within the historical framework, and he himself previously lived in one of the most beautiful Louis XV houses in Paris. For the last few years, however, he has lived on the top floor of a building near the American Church on the quai d' Orsay, where he can look out across the Seine to the Right Bank. His offices occupy the ground floor, and they are piled high with swatches of fabric and samples of furniture and boiseries from his own ateliers.

An elevator opens directly into his apartment. The eye is immediately dazzled by the lustrous sheen of metal: a statue by Hiquily, copper benches by the same artist, bronze ashtrays and cigarette urns by César, a low Lucite table with a metal border by Rougemont. Neon lights spread a soft glow under the tabletop, and a tubular sculpture by Ron Ferri glows beyond the entrance to the dining room. The shock of metal comes, too, in the salon from an elaborate Empire fireplace rich with caryatids and decorations in bronze doré. Over the mantel hangs a masterpiece by Balthus, an artist who, working quite apart from any accepted modern movement, is already beginning to be considered one of France's finest painters.

The dining room is an extension of the living room, a large alcove with simple Louis XVI chairs. The color scheme evolves from a ceiling painting. Representing the heavens with all the signs of the zodiac, it is the work of the Spanish artist Borés, who has lived in France for forty years. A library further extends the salon into the interior of the apartment. It is alive with a vibrant contemporary spirit, and adorning the walls are objects rather than paintings: a collage and a windowshade by Aeschbacher, a young Swiss artist, and a Calder mobile. There are low chairs and an amusing sofa by Arnal that rests on four half-spheres of plastic.

The difference between Henri Samuel's apartment in Paris and his country retreat is the difference between a cocktail party that brings together glittering people from here and there and everywhere—and a cozy family gathering. Montfort-l'Amaury is an enchanting little town some thirty miles south of Paris. There, many years ago, Henri Samuel bought an unpretentious house located near the old village walls. It was built at the end of the eighteenth century, remodeled around 1830 and is in the middle of a small, romantic park. The house contains a mixture of furniture, the kind passed down from one generation to the next and characteristic of every French village. Nevertheless, it has all been chosen with a great deal of care. The armoires were inherited from a cousin renowned for making excellent jams and preserves; there are tables from a grandmother who was the brightest light in her small town; there are bibelots from uncles who, in their time, had traveled as far as Switzerland, Italy—and even Turkey.

The sitting room is quite frankly in the exuberant style of Napoleon III, and the dining room is Directoire, a pleasant place in which to pass the unhurried hours enjoying delicious cuisine in the country manner. In the guest rooms there are wallcoverings of *toile de Gênes,* more than one hundred years old, gay with flowering trees and fantastic birds. Portraits, nostalgic scenes of country life and flower prints adorn the walls.

The master bedroom is decorated with Chinese fabric, since the focal point is an English bed done in that curious affectation made popular by the Prince Regent at the Brighton Pavilion. Windows overlook the garden, and it requires very little imagination to visualize elegant ladies in hoop skirts, like those painted by Monet and Boudin, playing hide-and-seek among the lilac bushes.

Is there any need to say that Henri Samuel is a happy man, a man with that contented face so often found in eighteenth-century portraits? He has achieved the golden mean, a life balanced between opposites: a city life, worldly and creative and open to experiment, and a country life devoted to repose and the pleasures of memory.

PARIS APARTMENT

The evening sky, the Seine and the Right Bank shine softly outside designer Henri Samuel's Paris apartment. Modern paintings by Balthus, Léger, Jawlensky and Christo, and contemporary furnishings by Guy de Rougemont and Arnal, are combined with traditional Louis XVI pieces.

OPPOSITE: *Candlelight and Ron Ferri's neon sculpture set the contemporary polished metal-topped Dining Room table aglow. Richard Lindner's painting overlooks the stylized blend of contemporary and antique elements; a mural by Borés depicts the heavens and signs of the zodiac.*

RIGHT: *In the Salon, a discreet background—created by neutral wall tones, textured upholstery and a rug with a trompe l'oeil geometric pattern—permits the contrasting collections of paintings and antiquities, Louis XVI furniture and unusual contemporary designs to coexist. The large polished metal and laminated plastic table was designed by Guy de Rougemont.*

COUNTRY HOUSE

*Henri Samuel's country house at Montfort
d'Amaury, thirty miles south of Paris, is situated
in a romantic, parklike setting. Built at the end of
the 18th century near the walls of the old village, it
was remodeled in 1830. Like most French country
homes, it is filled with a mixture of furnishings,
most of which have been passed down from one
generation of M. Samuel's family to the next.*

Floral motifs accent the Living Room: Bouquets from the garden fill the vases; the 19th-century moquette rug is patterned with roses; bellpull and drapery borders are flowered; prints and paintings carry on the theme. A pair of English Regency chairs flanks the book-laden Empire table, while a collection of boxes and objects in mother-of-pearl and gilt bronze share a mahogany tabletop.

Another view of the Living Room reveals the balanced arrangement of furnishings and art objects. Against the light-paneled far wall, scenes of country life and pastels border a large gilt-framed mirror. Tufted sofas and Louis XVI velvet-covered chairs surround a marble intarsia-topped table.

*In the Master Bedroom,
chinoiserie-inspired chintz based on
a 19th-century document print
covers the canopied English Regency
bed and is repeated in the chair
upholstery and draperies. The
unusual lampshade near the bed is
decorated with a fixé, in this case
oil painting, on mirror. The rug is
an antique Samarkand. Tall
windows overlook the large garden.*

The design of the Jardin d'Hiver celebrates the exuberant style of the Second Empire. Palms and other plants merge with the exotic mélange of trees and birds on the antique print wallcovering. The Victorian rug and bamboo furniture complement an amusing Napoleon III tête-à-tête.

149

HELLENIC PURITY OF FORM

The influence of the late T. H. Robsjohn-Gibbings has been, and will remain, a seminal one in the field of interior design. And his contributions to good taste in general will long be felt as well. In addition to being known for his unique contributions to contemporary design, he was also admired for his witty and provocative books on the subject. Literary and visual talents do not often go hand in hand, but he had a full measure of both.

There are few present-day designers, whether in Europe or the United States, who do not acknowledge some debt to his vision and to the efforts he made to simplify, to his rejection of decorative excesses, and to his insistence on quality and comfort and the harmony of design.

Born in England, T. H. Robsjohn-Gibbings lived and worked for many years in the United States, of which he became a citizen. In the last period of his life he moved to Greece, where he divided his time between an apartment in Athens and a villa on one of the Greek islands, continuing as always to design and to write with great flair and a clear grasp of contemporary life.

His talent was based, not only on a sense of the appropriate and an exquisite sense of humor, but on careful scholarship and an extensive knowledge of all periods and styles of interior design. To the end he continued to express—charmingly and devastatingly, as was his habit—his disdain for the awkward and the maudlin and the ungracious, both in design and in life. His views changed little since the days when he wrote those delightful, and at the time iconoclastic, books *Mona Lisa's Mustache, Homes of the Brave* and *Goodbye, Mr. Chippendale.*

"The world," he was fond of saying, "progresses by the strength of the individual." His own interests ranged widely over many different areas of art and design, and he counted among those who influenced him the architect Frank Lloyd Wright and a number of contemporary painters. Above all, however, he maintained his own particular identity and was true to his own particular vision. He believed that—in design, in art, in literature, in life itself—the simplest strokes are the boldest. It follows that what he left out of a design was quite as important as what he included.

The ephemeral in design was something that always displeased him, and for this reason much of his early work is as fresh today as it was when originally conceived. The famous chairs, based on the ancient Greek klismos, that he designed more than forty years ago are as striking now as they were then. Because they have the eternal quality that interested him so much in every phase of his design career, they are as much at home in the chrome and Lucite décor of the contemporary environment as they are in more traditional surroundings.

Indeed, a stunning mixture of the new and the old, of the natural and the man-made, of the traditional and the avant-garde, has always marked a Robsjohn-Gibbings interior. Nothing he ever designed was meant to reflect the fashion of the moment. If it were possible, or desirable, to define his approach to interior design in a single word, that word would be *classical*. The word surely suggests his unwavering belief in quality and his complete devotion to purity of form and design.

"It's a curious thing about Americans," he said. "They have an extraordinary open-mindedness about what is new. They're quite willing to consider and to accept the latest of everything. That's splendid, but it can also be very dangerous. It is too easy to fall into the trap of the ephemeral."

His own originality meant little to Robsjohn-Gibbings, and his major concern was always for the continuity of good design principles. "He was able to create practically anything," says his longtime design associate Carlton W. Pullin. "He brought his unique vision not only to interiors but to furniture and jewelry as well." And perhaps there is nowhere that the purity and versatility of his approach can be seen to better advantage than in the Athens apartment where he spent his last years. It is a summary of the man and the designer, a gathering together of tastefully and carefully chosen objects—all reflecting a lifelong devotion to simplicity in design and to the understanding of form and space. To see what is left out and what is included, to consider the pre-

cision and the elegance, is to gain some insight into Robsjohn-Gibbings's methods. The lesson of simplicity, too often overlooked by nonprofessionals as well as by many designers themselves, is an extremely compelling one.

The apartment, situated in what he described as "not a very smart section of Athens," is less than a block from the Parthenon—one of the ultimate signatures of the classical past and a fitting symbol of T. H. Robsjohn-Gibbings's approach to design. It combines the best of the old and the new.

There are a number of antiquities scattered throughout the apartment: a small plaque, for example, on the living room wall with two pieces of stone from the Parthenon, rescued from a scrap pile during some excavations on the Acropolis; and a marble lion's foot from Delos. These fragments of the ancient world harmonize perfectly with the white lacquered chairs he designed after Greek models of the fifth century B.C. The color scheme of the apartment is neutral and simple, with beige tones predominating. It makes a fitting background for the many pieces of rustic Greek basketry and wickerwork that are found throughout, in the entrance hall particularly. Simplicity is the keynote, but it is far from artless. There is no room for error, since there are no distractions of color or complex fabrics or innumerable furnishings. Proportion, space and harmony have all been carefully considered and organized by the hand of a master.

"Consider the alternative to the endless scramble for ostentation," wrote Robsjohn-Gibbings in one of his last articles: "No compulsion from state, society or fashion can force a living soul to be other than himself inside the one toehold he has on this planet—his home. In equipping a house, every individual choice, regardless of money or effort, will reveal completely the likeness of the inhabitants. This all-revealing factor cannot be evaded, cheated or bought off by ostentation."

T. H. Robsjohn-Gibbings followed his own quest for purity and classicism and intelligence to the end—joyfully and with his characteristic impatience with the shoddy and the ostentatious.

BELOW: *During his final years, the late T. H. Robsjohn-Gibbings lived in an Athens apartment located less than a block from the Parthenon. It was an apt setting for a designer/writer who drew inspiration from the simplicity and purity of Greece's Golden Age.*

OPPOSITE: *Objects indigenous to the Greek islands and countryside are discriminatingly positioned against clear space. In the foreground is a wicker buoy; behind it, a Skyros shepherd's crook and wooden beaters used for washing clothes in the sea. Donkey beads festoon a pony skull traditionally believed to ward off the evil eye. A clay jug and a wooden churn complete the arrangement of rustic utilitarian devices.*

FAR RIGHT: *In 1934, Robsjohn-Gibbings designed these white-lacquered, leather-thong-seated chairs, reviving the 6th-century B.C. klismos. They were later fabricated as part of his collection of twenty-six pieces based on Greek models.*

BELOW: *In the Living Room, vibrant gladiolus in a Pentelic marble bowl repeat the floral motifs adorning a contemporary Greek silk tapestry and a delicately carved and painted 18th-century Greek dower chest. Adding vertical thrust is a Greek wrought-iron candleholder.*

OPPOSITE: *Robsjohn-Gibbings's classically inspired furniture designs exist harmoniously among the uncluttered spaces of the Living Room. An archaic Greek lion, a framed 18th-century Ottoman Empire edict and engravings by Louis Dupré impart a sense of history.*

OPULENT ECLECTICISM IN LONDON

Less may be more, and opulence may have been shunned by those who feel it has not been entirely fashionable for some time now, but sumptuous materials will always be seductive and there will always be those who prefer luxurious living over fashion trends. "The house laughs bright with silver" is a description once made by the Roman poet Horace of a house readied for festivity. Persian palaces, the Byzantine court, the palaces of the Moguls—each brings to mind dreams of walls encrusted with jewels and semiprecious stones and covered with silver, ivory and mother-of-pearl.

Antony Redmile is an inheritor of this opulent tradition. His designs for furniture and decorative objects are rich with silver, ivory, malachite, carnelian and amethyst, and his own house, in London, is sheer exuberant luxury.

He respects, and is much influenced by, the timelessness of all fine things. Proportions and shapes—even humor—will endure if the quality is there, and he adheres to certain strict rules of his own devising. His special style is taken very seriously, and deservedly so, for he is a most unique designer. It must be said, however, that Mr. Redmile's occasional follies do make him vulnerable to criticism from those who would define "serious" in other terms. For example, he once designed a container for after-dinner mints that was made from a hinged human skull. He hastens to explain that the skull had once been used by Tibetan monks as a begging bowl. Therefore it is an antique, an object with that sense of the past he so ardently seeks. The humor is individual; the rules and logic are completely his own.

There is the same logic, even inevitability, in the way he acquired his pet boa constrictor. He had promised to look after it for a friend who was going on holiday. But the friend never claimed it, so Antony Redmile began to build a proper cage: a twelve-foot-high silver chalice with an onion dome, the whole inlaid with malachite and set on a silver palm tree with a base of amethysts.

He has both sophisticated common sense and a naïve enthusiasm for the fantastic. Many would label him decadent, but he surely does not seek decadence. His grounding in good solid design is too strong, and he makes a very clear distinction between the grotesque and the macabre. He dotes on the former and totally rejects the latter.

Mr. Redmile is not in the habit of decorating entire houses, although often enough—as with the presidential palace at Malawi, with its skulls of African animals, its ivory and semiprecious stones—his contributions have been dominant.

"My own house is not a decorator's house," he says adamantly. "I only wanted a neutral background for the objects I design."

Although the sitting room does have plain, pale walls and carpet, the other rooms are highly decorated and can scarcely be called neutral. The bath, for example, is a glittering cave of tiny mirrored tiles on every surface, curved or flat, reflecting and refracting light until the small space seems the very heart of a treasure den.

The bedroom is dominated by a large mural that he painted himself, the classical motif taken from a vase excavated at Paestum. The dining room, too, has a mural that he and a friend painted: a peaceful Italian Renaissance loggia; beyond its arches, a serene and gentle landscape.

"Originally I had painted heads leering from behind the arches," Mr. Redmile recalls, "and they stared out at my dinner guests. This did seem a trifle bizarre, however, and they were painted out."

No, it is definitely not a neutral house, and Antony Redmile's designs are not the sort that people feel neutral about, either. The word *perhaps* has possibly never been spoken in his shop. One day Jacqueline Onassis walked in and could not resist sketching everything. And she did, it must be added, order a considerable amount at a later date. Now Middle Eastern sheikhs come and negotiate prices. And even the English are beginning to appreciate the beauty of his work.

"Horn chandeliers were the sort of things that grandmother had in the house in Scotland," says Mr. Redmile. "Invariably the heirs threw such things out, but now they wish they'd kept them."

He travels often and extensively, seeing people and being stimulated by the arts of earlier civilizations, particularly those of the Far East and Egypt and Mexico. The raw materials he usually finds at home, many of them hunting trophies long forgotten in the attics of country houses. It must be remembered that he is one of the sponsors of the Preservation of Wildlife Committee, and he is quick to point out that all his tusks and horns and furs are antiques. Pheasant feathers are the pluckings from the poultry department at Harrods, and the ostrich eggs come from special farms. In the designer's workshops some forty craftsmen use metal, wood, pottery, seashells and paint to combine the antique and the modern—to produce furniture and chandeliers and varied objects that go to shops and decorators in every part of the world.

Caution is definitely put to one side and fantasy reigns when he has some special exhibition. One Easter in London, for example, he made a remarkable four-poster bed, the posts themselves being narwhal tusks, the spiral horn attributed to the legendary unicorn, and the canopy of silver set with ostrich eggs. Thinking this confection not arresting enough, he added the involved boa constrictor cage to the exhibition, along with his own vintage Rolls-Royce. It will come as no surprise to learn that the motor car was covered with seashells.

The house in which he lives and the dramatically bizarre objects within it change constantly. When he originally bought the house, it was, as he says, nothing more than a "typical London lodging house." Many of the initial changes he made, such as the addition of a modern wooden staircase, seem out of character to him now. With that characteristic blend of high seriousness and genial good humor, he is considering a number of alterations that strike him as being more appropriate today. He thinks he might start with the staircase.

"I could cover it with ivory and malachite," he muses. "Or I could simply take it all out and then I could begin from the beginning."

Whatever the decision, be certain that *anything* is possible with Antony Redmile.

LEFT: *Painted stone dogs and a Spanish-style star lamp enliven the entrance to the typically London townhouse, built circa 1840, of designer Antony Redmile.* OPPOSITE: *In the Dining Room, the horned skull of an Ethiopian sheep and a semicircular antler chandelier, together with a pair of grotesque masklike sconces, establish the keynote—at once naturalistic and bizarre—of an unusual and sumptuous interior. A mirrored wall restates a handsome William Kent eagle console and dramatically extends the illusion created by a trompe l'oeil mural depicting an Italian Renaissance loggia and a pastoral landscape.*

In the Sitting Room, neutral tones offset prized objects—many created by the designer himself. A glass-topped table houses a Victorian seashell collection, while enormous elephant tusks form parentheses around an arrangement of Japanese porcelain skulls and Egyptian statuary.

Mr. Redmile adds his distinctive touch even to objects he has not designed, by creating unusual settings for them: He placed a 16th-century blanc de chine figure of Kuan-Yin before a semicircular metal panel, originally from a lighthouse, that creates surreal reflections of the object.

LEFT: *The mural Mr. Redmile painted for the Master Bedroom is based on a motif from a Greek vase excavated at Paestum. On the ceiling, arranged like the spokes of a wheel, fifty 18th-century Indian tulwars surround a gleaming antique "witch ball"; still others radiate from the corners of the room. In the foreground is another of the designer's unique assemblages—an 18th-century Italian carved monkey surmounted by a ceramic clamshell lamp.* OPPOSITE: *Tiny mirrors glisten throughout the Bath, where a dozen ostrich eggs comprise an exotic chandelier.*

VENETIAN FANTASY IN PUERTO VALLARTA

For centuries the phoenix, the legendary bird that rises from its own destruction, has fascinated poets and painters and writers. Now part of mythology, it is the symbol that inspired Hasi Hester's unusual home on the beach at Puerto Vallarta.

As a matter of fact, Mr. Hester—whose fabric and furniture showroom is well-known in Los Angeles—was guided by three separate enthusiasms in the creation of a dramatic and, at first glance, incongruous residence. Like so many before him, he was attracted by the lure of Mexico itself; he has a special affection for the Gothic magnificence of Venetian architecture; and he holds a firm, and personal, belief in the legend of the phoenix.

That these widely different elements have been combined with elegance and authority is the triumph of *Palazzo Fenice*. Perhaps it is strange to find what is essentially a small Venetian palace named after the phoenix on Conchas Chinas beach in Puerto Vallarta. But it does not seem strange to Hasi Hester nor to the many friends and clients who have visited him in this enchanted setting.

"It's my small corner of peace," says Mr. Hester. "The world outside can get hectic, and the beauty I find here is as rare as the time to enjoy it."

Perhaps more important is the fact that Puerto Vallarta has a very special meaning for him. He has come here often over the years and during that time has seen a village of five thousand people—and three automobiles—turn into a resort with a population that now numbers more than sixty thousand.

Some time ago, after a serious accident, he instinctively returned to Puerto Vallarta in order to recuperate—to swim in the ocean and to ride horseback along the beach. His recovery was almost miraculous, and he knew then that he had to have a house of his own there. And, with his head full of visions of Venice and a personal identification with the legend of the phoenix, he knew the sort of house he wanted and even what the name was going to be: "I had the whole thing completed in my mind long before I ever actually saw it." The day came when he found exactly what he was looking for. The house, he will admit, was the "ugliest in Puerto Vallarta," but it had the right location and the right feeling. When he looked at it, he did not see the house as it existed—but, rather, an image of the completed Palazzo Fenice.

"I had the pleasure of seeing a fantasy fulfilled," says Mr. Hester, "in one of the few places in the world where it all could have happened."

Little is taken amiss in Mexico, and the Latin temperament accepts the amiable eccentricities of foreigners with a good deal of tolerance. If the *señor norteamericano* wanted a Venetian palace, there was very little reason why he should not have it. To turn the vision into reality, however, was quite another matter. First of all, it involved taking the house down to its foundation and starting from the beginning. Surprisingly, the lot itself is not unlike a site in Venice—long, narrow, located between the road and the water, the house high and multistoried with a small garden behind.

Working with architect Jim Meares and consulting his own extensive library of books on Venetian architecture, Hasi Hester selected the arches and columns and doors he wanted to duplicate. The octagonal living room, for example, has large open arches on each of the eight sides under an eighteen-foot cupola. And over and over again the predominant theme of the house is joyfully repeated: Let the outside in.

Remodeling was accomplished in less than six months, and it seems a remarkable achievement, given the extensive renovation required. And it is generally accepted that things are not rushed in Mexico; however, Mr. Hester has nothing but admiration for the team of local artisans who carved the stone columns and carefully duplicated the doors and stairways of another civilization. Although that civilization may seem far removed from modern Mexico, the house that rose from the ruins of the old is strangely appropriate. The small Venetian palace by no means seems out of place in Puerto Vallarta. Oddly enough, Spanish Colonial architecture does carry with it some echoes of Venice. Indeed, the very bricks—made only in this part of Mexico—give the house, in Hasi Hester's

words, "a marvelous pink terra-cotta color, very Venetian in feeling, with the same quality of light."

Naturally Mr. Hester wanted to bring the outside into his house and to have no rigid boundaries between the natural and the man-made. The whole was to be one harmonious unit—the sea and the garden and the sky flowing back and forth through arches supported by columns and topped by soaring domes. These great open arches—and the fact that most of the interior is filled with plants—illustrates the graceful way in which Hasi Hester has made the most of the natural setting. "You know, my idea of the perfect room is a lush garden with lots of comfortable chairs around," he says. And this is precisely the feeling he has created in the Palazzo Fenice. Much of the charm of the alfresco atmosphere was made possible, he feels, by the work of his good friend Gabriel Urrutia who did the landscape architecture.

It is no wonder that the owner and his friends return time and again to this magical setting. Everything has been irresistibly arranged to give the illusion of living outside, on the beach or in the garden. Perhaps the most entrancing moment of all is the dinner hour in a brick pavilion near the beach, surrounded by the ocean and the stars.

"This is my little island," says Hasi Hester with obvious contentment. "A lovely setting of fantasy where my friends and I can keep the world at bay. Part of the pleasure, I suppose, is knowing I have a house that will never really be finished."

His vision of the phoenix is without end; there are more fantasies to be realized, and a comfortable and imaginative house will continue to weave a spell of unexplained magic. Magic? Yes, there are not many places in the world where it is possible to walk through a small English garden to the beach, to ride white Arabian horses on the sand with a Venetian palace in the background. From the purist's point of view nothing is right, but everything does seem to work splendidly. The Palazzo Fenice most definitely is—in the words of an Italian critic describing the Doge's Palace in Venice—"a miracle of illogical coherence."

An iron sculpture of the mythical phoenix—after which Mr. Hasi Hester's Palazzo Fenice *is named—surmounts the entrance gate from Conchas Chinas beach at Puerto Vallarta. Behind the enclosing wall and past the Gothic-arched gate, banks of greenery cascade from tiers of colonnaded porches, culminating in an eighteen-foot octagonal cupola inspired by Venetian palace architecture.*

A stairway ascends the terraced garden lush with tropical foliage. Variously colored croton, dracaena, ficus, poinciana and portulaca merge with the ferns, petunias and bougainvillea planted on each of the open porches, integrating the unusual architecture with the vigorous oceanside environment.

Sweeping arches open the periphery of the octagonally shaped Living Room and frame views of adjacent areas. French-style furniture adds a formal element to the predominantly natural atmosphere created by brick walls, tiled floor, earth-toned dome and potted plants. A floral still life by Mexican painter Tellosa and vases of garden flowers interject bright colors.

Graceful palms and other leafy foliage echo the curve of an arch spanning a view of the Living Room from the Dining Area. The rustic chairs, covered in pigskin, have been designed in the same manner for many centuries. A painting by Vidali depicts the relaxed life enjoyed in Puerto Vallarta.

BELOW LEFT: *Hand-carved Venetian-style columns of locally quarried stone flank the entrance to the Master Bath. Fluted columns, topped with greenery-filled urns, define the boundaries of a glass-walled shower.*

LOWER LEFT: *A Gothic-style archway leads to a Guest Bath. Nearby, a 16th-century santo stands on an antique Mexican mirrored cabinet.* BELOW RIGHT: *A fanciful mirror in another Bath repeats the arches of a Guest Room.*

OPPOSITE: *Like a deep pool of water, the dark polished surface of the Master Bedroom's tiled floor restates the painted bamboo bed. Engravings are 16th and 17th century; the pastel is from the School of Fragonard.*

LEFT: *The Loggia of the "Lido" guest suite is open to the tropical environment, especially to the cooling ocean breezes wafting in from the beach. Rough-textured and porous local stone was used to form the columns and arches that define the space. Pigskin-upholstered chairs, identical to those in the dining area, and a glass-topped iron table encourage dining alfresco.* OPPOSITE: *A graceful colonnade is silhouetted against the clear blue water of the Bahia de Banderas as it stretches into the Pacific Ocean.*

CHATEAU DE LA CHAIZE—A TRIBUTE TO TRADITION IN BEAUJOLAIS

The French are inclined to spend far less time in their châteaux than the English do in their country houses. Most of them only go from time to time to oversee the land, in the fall for the hunting and now and then for short holidays.

As it is everywhere, help is difficult to find, and, too, heating the large châteaux has become economically unfeasible. Such expenses present few problems in historic châteaux visited by thousands of tourists annually, but they are a serious consideration for the owners of private châteaux.

Many families have been forced to spend money they can ill afford in order to maintain these heritages of the past, and others have sold paintings and antique furniture and even boiseries from the walls. Unless such houses are designated historic monuments, the process of decay is inevitable.

It requires a good deal of productive land for an estate to be maintained in the manner it was a hundred years ago. Vineyards, for example, make it possible for the Marquise de Roussy de Sales to keep the château she inherited some years ago in excellent condition. Her wine is a Côte de Brouilly, a renowned Beaujolais stored in enormous casks above vaulted cellars stretching underground in an endless perspective. Cases of the wine are shipped to every part of the world—the bottles bearing a label that depicts the *Château de la Chaize* surrounded by its vineyards.

Originally the estate belonged to François d'Aix, nephew of the important Jesuit priest, Père La Chaize, who was confessor to Louis XIV. Construction of the château began in 1676 and was completed in only two years—a fact explaining its remarkable uniformity of design. The architecture is attributed to Jules Mansart; and the arrangement of the gardens, to André Le Nôtre. Both men worked extensively at Versailles.

The château—with its ochre-colored stone, glazed roof tiles, white shutters and sunny terrace—presents such an enchanting aspect that its enormous dimensions are often overlooked. From the terrace, surrounded in summer by orange trees in white pots, there is a view embracing the whole

174

region of Brouilly, its sloping hills covered with vines. On a clear day the Alps loom in the distance.

High iron gates leading into the courtyard are painted blue in the seventeenth-century manner, and a flight of steps leads to a heavy oak door opening into an enormous hall filled with fluted columns. Animal heads carved above the capitals are repeated in the coat of arms of the owners of the château. Rising from this imposing entrance hall is a staircase whose walls are lined with portraits of owners who followed François d'Aix de La Chaize: members of the Montaigu family—a succession of generals, ambassadors and princes of the church.

The last Marquise de Montaigu was a famous turn-of-the-century beauty, and she eventually left the château to her niece Nicole, an elegant young lady whose husband is director of Dior perfumes. Despite the stern portraits of religious figures in the house, no one could be less austere than Nicole de Roussy herself. And, being a woman of great taste and intelligence, she has had the good sense to preserve the imposing atmosphere of the château, while making it exceedingly comfortable.

To create the desired effect, she sought the help of Parisian interior designer Jean Paul Faye, who is known both for his talent and his immense tact. Together they succeeded in completely transforming a large and rather sad house, overloaded with miscellaneous bric-a-brac and much furniture collected through the centuries. The first steps were to eliminate everything that did not harmonize with the splendid boiseries, to restore the paintings, to create private apartments for the owners and, little by little, to refurbish the guest rooms.

Happily, the attic was a treasure house of antique furniture, the style thought to be outmoded a century ago but eagerly collected today. There were, for example, many fine Louis XVI pieces signed by Jacob that Jean Paul Faye arranged in the salon, brightening the room by bleaching the furniture and covering it with white and rose fabric. Along with mahogany Empire beds there were endless clocks and vases and candlesticks. Everything was put to use to renovate the house.

Off a long gallery on the first floor are the owners' private apartments. The rooms of the marquis are furnished in a rather English manner with dark fabrics, while the marquise favors Louis XVI furniture in tones of white. On the second floor there are perhaps a dozen guest rooms, and on the third floor the children—three girls and a boy—have charming rooms with small-paned windows and wallpaper painted in 1830. One of the loveliest rooms of all belongs to the English governess.

In actual fact, what sort of life is led in the château today? It is a very restful one, indeed—except for the lady of the house. The Marquise de Roussy can be found early each day in the hall arranging bouquets in vases on a large table, panniers of flowers at her feet and her children often helping. She selects the flowers herself from the rose garden or from the herbaceous borders surrounding four sides of the parterre.

A little before luncheon a bell rings, and it is the custom to meet on the terrace for an aperitif under the shade of an immense linden tree. Before long a second bell rings, and luncheon is served in the dining room. Later it is almost impossible not to climb the staircase to one of the guest rooms for a nap or to read the memoirs that fill the bookshelves of the château—memoirs often mentioning the experiences of other guests who have stayed at La Chaize in the past. In the afternoon visits are made to neighboring houses or to one of the Romanesque churches so characteristic of the area. Soon it is time to return to dress for cocktails and dinner.

This enchanting way of life is organized without apparent effort by Nicole de Roussy—but nothing is left to chance. Everything goes smoothly because, even in winter, she visits La Chaize at least twice a month to see that all is in order.

At La Chaize a young lady, soigné and determined, made up her mind to live in the manner of her ancestors, yet with contemporary ease and comfort. M. Faye understood her wishes completely, and today the Château de la Chaize is as comfortable as can be, at the same time retaining all the delicious qualities of a vanished century.

LEFT: *Five hundred acres of park and fertile Beaujolais vineyards surround the* Château de la Chaize, *the 17th-century country home of the Marquise de Roussy de Sales. Weathered stone walls and stately iron gates enclose a formal garden landscaped with topiary shrubs.*

OPPOSITE: *Massive oak doors open into an imposing Entrance Hall, characterized by the same classical symmetry that defines the exterior. Fluted columns crowned by sculpted heads of hounds punctuate the vast, stone-floored expanse. A rounded arch, set between a pair of arched and mirrored doorways, frames the main staircase. Like a precious jewel in a fine setting, an intricately carved and gilded Régence console occupies a position of importance at the landing.*

OPPOSITE: *Designer Jean Paul Faye chose related hues for the Salon's Louis XVI boiserie, creating a subtle geometric background for family portraits. Graceful Louis XV consoles flank the fireplace—a counterpoint to the classically straight lines of a pair of Louis XVI canapés.*

RIGHT: *An Empire crystal chandelier softly lights the Dining Room, where scenic panels painted by Lacroix de Marseille alternate with vividly draped and valanced French doors. The damask tablecloth bears the coat of arms of the Marquise's ancestors, the Montaigu family.*

LEFT: *Painted figures repose against the trompe l'oeil ceiling molding in the Chambre du Roi, creating the illusion of marble carvings. The walls, covered with Restoration wallpaper, resemble draperies enriched with lambrequins.*

LEFT: *Imari covered jars and a bouquet of garden flowers accent the Chambre du Roi's architectonic Louis XIV marble mantel, the focal point of a seating arrangement comprised of a Louis XV chaise longue and bergère.*

Light-painted Restoration boiserie, warm accents,
bright floral fabric and country furniture
harmonize in one of the château's dozen or so Guest
Rooms. A Venetian chandelier reinforces the sense
of delicacy while emphasizing a lofty ceiling.

A pair of demilune overdoor mirrors enhances the geometry of the boiserie in another Guest Room. The marble mantel is graced—in traditional fashion—with an antique clock, a gilt-framed mirror and symmetrically placed vases and jars.

A second pair of demilune overdoor mirrors in the Guest Room reiterates the curve of a sleeping alcove upholstered in a light, leafy fabric. Dark flooring and dark wood furniture purposefully underscore the room's dominant airiness.

Louis XIV's architect, Jules Mansart, is credited with designing the château, which features a typical mansard-hipped roof and a pedimented and pilastered façade. The original arrangement of the extensive gardens is attributed to the king's favorite landscape gardener, André Le Nôtre.

TUNISIAN
SANCTUARY

The rhythmic movement of the surf, the sighing of the wind in the palm trees, the humming of bees among the orange blossoms—these are the sounds of Hammamet. It is a Moorish village on the northern coast of Tunisia, happily removed from the busy world and its pressures. In such a setting it is inevitable that the senses be lulled into a state of almost constant euphoria. It is a dream world, where breakfast is enjoyed on a sun-drenched balcony, luncheon in the cool shade of a loggia, dinner by the light of flaming torches—and all around are the mysteriously evocative remains of many an ancient civilization.

Dar Saouari is a villa in Hammamet quite as real as it is dreamlike in the atmosphere it projects. Built by Claudio Bruni Sakraischik and Stanley John Allen—the owners of La Medusa, a distinguished modern art gallery in Rome—the villa very nearly did not come into being.

"When I first traveled in Tunisia," says Claudio Sakraischik, "it was in the winter. I had the unhappy impression that the whole country was little more than a desert. Quite obviously that first impression was very far from the truth."

Indeed, it was. The coastal areas of Tunisia have much the same climate and much of the same lush greenness as other Mediterranean littorals. He and Stanley Allen soon decided that Hammamet would be the ideal place to build a house.

"We chose Hammamet in particular," explains Claudio Sakraischik, "because it is one of those rarities in the world today, an unspoiled village that nevertheless has all the necessary amenities for comfortable living. We decided to build on the beach rather than in the medina, because our other houses—one in Rome's Trastevere section and the other a country place near Lake Bracciano—are quite landlocked."

When it came to selecting a building site, the problem was easily resolved. There was only one plot available: an orange grove measuring 2,000 square meters. With a lot so relatively small, the obvious solution was to build the house in the center. The idea of a small house on small grounds was not particularly appealing, however, and Stanley Allen had a better idea: "Why not reverse the usual procedure by building the house around the property and leaving the center open?" This plan was followed, and the result is that the house is now one of the largest in the immediate area. Surely it has the most spacious court.

While digging the foundations, workmen uncovered many authentic treasures of the past. They found, for example, some twenty columns and a statue, all intact—the remains of a Roman temple that had once stood on the spot. These relics of the past were placed in the garden, possibly in the exact location where they stood when this part of Africa was temporarily under Roman rule.

The exterior plan of Dar Saouari—"The House of the Columns" in Arabic—is in complete harmony with its setting. Cube-shaped and dazzling white, with domes rising above the roof line, it nestles among shrubs and trees and lawn—a collage of white and green and sky blue. In one corner of the complex stands a *marabout,* a tiny domed structure used as a guesthouse. In earlier times the *marabout* was the domain of the watchman, usually a retired thief who, because of his many connections, was able to ensure his owner against robbery. Such buildings are scattered all over Tunisia.

"In the context of a thoroughly Moorish house," says Claudio Sakraischik, "I thought it would be effective to have a contemporary European interior. But naturally there are Moorish details incorporated into the general scheme."

There is certainly no conflict at all with the North African setting. If anything, the contemporary treatment is a simplified version of ancient designs, and the décor reflects the many colors and involved geometry of Islamic architecture. Walls throughout the interior are white, and the floors are composed of gray-white marble—rectangular blocks for the interior and irregularly shaped pieces for the loggias. Marble is also used extensively in the baths, where there are sunken bathtubs the size of small swimming pools. Cross ventilation has assured cool temperatures, even though the North African sun burns overhead. Plans for the house were carefully drawn, and everything was considered before actual building began.

"I'm certainly not an architect," says Claudio Sakraischik, "but I decided to do some experimenting for Dar Saouari. When it came to designing the living and dining area, I wanted to put a large ceiling dome above the space that divides them. Not the usual sort of dome, built on a square and a hexagon, but one that would give the impression of floating in the air, something without any apparent means of support. I wasn't at all sure that my idea would work in the last analysis, and I was quite prepared to abandon the whole thing if it didn't. But, fortunately, it all worked out, and now architects occasionally come and ask *me* how it was done! I had the luck of ignorance, I suppose."

It will perhaps come as something of a surprise to find that there are no paintings at all on the walls of Dar Saouari, the home of prominent gallery owners. Indeed, La Medusa in Rome was one of the first galleries there to show the work of such American artists as Jackson Pollock, to introduce Pop Art and the New Realists. It would not seem unlikely to find some stunning contemporary art in this North African villa. On the other hand, perhaps the absence of it is not too difficult to understand. For most of the year in Italy the owners of La Medusa live with art on all sides, and Dar Saouari provides a respite, a place of refreshment for the spirit. Simplicity and spareness, in fact, are the keynotes of the villa, and it has been purposely designed to offer few distractions from the tranquility and the beauty and the remoteness of Hammamet. The art here is of a different kind.

With the exception of the Roman statuary in the garden, the only art in the villa is the plaster cast of a sculptured figure by Boccioni, which rests on a plexiglass pedestal directly under the large central dome of the main living area.

"Our professional life in Rome revolves around painting and sculpture of all kinds," says Claudio Sakraischik. "Here things are different. The whole house is a work of sculpture."

BELOW: *Studded motifs embellish the doors leading into the vaulted Entrance. Relics from antiquity—a stone doorway from a Tunisian palace, a Roman mosaic and a sculptured Roman foot—add history's patina to the pristine architecture.*

The modern European flavor of the villa's interior contrasts with its Moorish exterior. In the Gallery, the domed ceiling, stackable furniture designed by Chilean painter Matta and a plaster cast of a 1913 Boccioni sculpture create a structurally surrealistic atmosphere.

A SETTING FOR
ART AND ANTIQUES
IN MADRID

Some fifteen years ago interior designer Duarte Pinto Coelho decided to rent an apartment in the enormous and decorative *Pinohermosa Palace* on the calle Don Pedro in Madrid. At that time the apartment, while its proportions were magnificent, was almost a total ruin. The last tenant had been a firm of photographers, and much of the space had been reserved for darkrooms. Despite the extensive reconstruction needed, the designer's friends advised him to take it without delay.

"You have only to fix up part of it," they said. "The rest you can turn into exhibition space and also have room for a picture gallery."

"I'm not as worried about fixing it up," said the designer, "as about the parties I have to give."

Within three months—two of them found him out of town—the huge apartment was totally restored, painted, carpeted and filled with furniture and tapestries. Baths, fireplaces, lamps, draperies, china—everything was ready and everything functioned perfectly. The apartment came to life, and the anticipated parties soon began.

One of Señor Pinto Coelho's most striking traits is the apparent ease with which he achieves results. Everything he undertakes seems simple, from completely decorating a house to making arrangements for an elegant party. This is no doubt thanks to his great capacity for work and his innate ability to give orders. There is every reason to believe that he was born to be a leader, and in some ways he is remarkably autocratic. But this trait is much softened by another, and perhaps contradictory, gift: his ability to get along with people of all sorts. He gives orders, and he knows how he wants things done. But, because of his charm, people carry out these orders with genuine pleasure.

Portuguese by birth, he lived for many years in Paris as a young man, and he spent a good deal of time in Madrid as well. In the end he decided to open a shop in the Spanish capital. Calling it Carpa, he specialized in interior decoration, antiques and modern art. The beginning was smooth enough, and the shop was soon a success. He began to receive professional recognition almost immediately. His friends always found him willing to help put a house or an apartment together. And gradually, almost without realizing it, he found himself familiar with that network of craftsmen and artisans so necessary to the interior designer.

This period of his career lasted for about three years, and Carpa became a popular meeting place in Madrid. It was a tiny shop with a basement where exhibitions of paintings were held, but there were also drinks and pleasant dinners, and tables and chairs appearing as if by magic. However, all of it could have been put into one of the rooms of the designer's present apartment—a place his friends affectionately call the "Palazzo Pinto."

Duarte Pinto Coelho stands in his red salon. Although all the rooms in the apartment have the same feeling of panache and comfort, this particular room—with its red-striped silk fabrics, its deep sofas on either side of the fireplace, its piano and bar—is particularly conducive to intimate conversation. It is a relaxed setting for a dialogue about his work and thoughts on design.

"Decoration has always interested me," he says. "I suppose I was born with a fondness for rearranging things. Even as a little boy, I saw how various members of my family constantly moved the furniture around. More often than not, rooms looked better when they had finished. But I really began my career when I arrived in Spain. In Paris I simply watched and learned.

"The main point to remember is that houses are to be lived in, and they must reflect the people who own them. It is important for the final result to enhance the owner and not the decorator. In fact, the decorator should do the very best he can—and then quietly disappear. The house or apartment should look as if he had never been there at all."

Naturally there have been many important influences that have shaped his tastes, and he singles some of them out with affection: "One I remember so well is Mme Schiaparelli's house. There was an incredible mixture of things, a great deal of bric-a-brac on all sides. But through it all shone the extraordinary personality of the owner. I was also a great admirer of Charles de Beistegui and of the way he could fix up a house to look as if it had been lived in for generations. From him I learned to appreciate and understand beautiful things. But I respect traditional European styles more than I agree with them. Some of them are rigid and extremely cold in their formality. I find them impersonal, with no relation to everyday life."

Among projects that have given him great pleasure is a house he has restored and furnished for Mr. and Mrs. Cornelius Vanderbilt Whitney in Trujillo, and a palace he decorated for the president of the Republic of Malawi. The project in Trujillo, a town some hundred miles southwest of Madrid at the foot of the Sierra de Guadalupe, is particularly successful. He worked closely with Mrs. Whitney, and together they transformed an almost ruined sixteenth-century house into a lovely mansion.

Others have followed the example of the Whitneys and have undertaken to rebuild old houses in Trujillo. The town itself is famous for having been the cradle of many of the conquistadores of the New World, and in the plaza there is a magnificent statue of Francisco Pizarro, conqueror of Peru. The writer and painter Fleur Cowles and the portrait painter Channing Hare have also reconstructed old palaces here. A number of Spaniards have done the same, and the town of Trujillo has awakened from the deep sleep of the centuries. A few miles outside the town Duarte Pinto Coelho has built a country house for himself, and it is a place where he can relax completely and put aside for the moment the demands of his profession.

One of his major characteristics, however, is his internationalism, and he is always on the move. There are few other people who could be so completely at home in so many different parts of the world. He is a traveler by preference and necessity, and wherever he happens to be, it would be difficult for him not to have a friend.

"Life," says designer Pinto Coelho, "has given me the delightful gift of a profession I love and work to do that is literally a pleasure. All I ask is a little more time to enjoy it all!"

Designer Duarte Pinto Coelho's grand-scale apartment in Madrid's Pinohermosa Palace *bears the attractive results of extensive renovation. The sixty-foot-long Music Room contains several arrangements of furniture, each with its own axis. On the far wall, an imposing 17th-century Spanish organ is flanked by Baroque consoles and gilt-framed mirrors. Identical tables displaying Chinese porcelain, Roman busts and carved wooden figures border the major seating area, while a collection of contemporary paintings contrasts with the room's antique appointments. The richly upholstered Spanish furnishings, velvet draperies, golden-toned damask wallcovering and profusion of antique rugs contribute to a feeling of luxury.*

Details of the Music Room focus on groupings of collectables. RIGHT: Seventeenth-century blanc de chine figures cluster in front of a Ch'ien Lung jardinière and a Japanese lacquer, silk and leather screen. FAR RIGHT: A Ch'ien Lung lamp casts light on an unusual collection of early-19th-century straw objects made in France and Spain by prisoners of war.

The Salon provides a warm setting for work or conversation. RIGHT: A Regénce bureau plat holds a Sèvres porcelain inkstand and two porcelaine de Paris figures. FAR RIGHT: Louis XVI chairs surround a damask-draped book table. An assortment of treasures includes luminous Chinese paintings on glass against the striped silk-covered wall, a Roman head and an Italian statue.

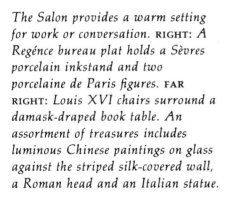

A Charles IV chandelier illuminates the vivid Salon. Chinese and European verre églomisé paintings are displayed on either side of the tortoiseshell mirror, and lapis lazuli columns enrich the mahogany bookcase. The trompe l'oeil ceiling restates the Neo-Classical pattern of the rug.

197

OPPOSITE: *Trompe l'oeil panels of laced and swagged drapery give an elegant, tentlike feeling to the unconventional twenty-seven-foot-long Dining Room. The boldly patterned Portuguese rug underlies a pair of Baroque-based tables and the Queen Anne-style Spanish chairs.*

BELOW: *The sophisticated Bath/Dressing Room is richly appointed in a 19th-century manner. Alabaster busts and statues decorate the marble mantel, while Empire opaline and crystal objects share a candlelit tabletop. Framed works include portraits of artists and of Señor Coelho.*

RIGHT: *A stairway leads to the Library's upper level, where guest room accommodations are concealed behind the bookshelves.* CENTER RIGHT: *Banquettes with lively patterned pillows bring contemporary comfort to the light-toned Library. Paintings hang against vinyl-covered walls from thin brass rods.* BELOW RIGHT: *A damask-draped writing table in the Master Bedroom holds an antique ebony and agate cabinet.* FAR RIGHT: *The 18th-century parquet floor of the Master Bedroom contrasts with the deep tones of the moiré wallcovering, velvet bedcovering and drapery, and small Oriental rug. Gilt objects—a Baroque column, a pair of consoles and 18th-century mirrors from Minorca—enrich the setting.*

AN ENGLISH ARCHITECT'S FARMHOUSE IN PROVENCE

It is heartwarming and perhaps unusual to find a house so exactly consistent with its setting as Thomas Wilson's three-hundred-year-old farmhouse in the Provence region.

Rising in mellow red from a luxuriant field of flowers, the farmhouse could be in no other place in the world. The atmosphere is perfect in every way. There are masses of anemones and groves of olive trees, and the original farmhouse door has been stripped back to its natural wood. On a stone terrace there is even a resident peahen. Because the effect is at once so carefully contrived and so lovingly authentic, it is difficult to imagine that much of the Impressionist aura of the house and its surrounding fields of flowers has been the work of a contemporary English architect.

In a truly Provençal manner, the scene is bucolic and unspoiled. The delicate scent of flowers is everywhere, coming from the endless fields of jasmine and roses and orange blossoms. For the farmhouse lies very near Grasse, the fragrance capital of the world, where the essences of the most exquisite perfumes are obtained. The old town of Grasse is quiet and rural, the streets narrow and the houses built with that rough-hewn masonry so characteristic of the district.

"Despite a feeling of remoteness," says Mr. Wilson, "Grasse is very central to other places on the Continent. I live five miles from the sea, and it's only an hour's drive to the mountains for skiing in the winter. There's a great deal to do, and many English and Americans live in the neighborhood—lured, I expect, both by the beauty of the countryside and by the marvelous convenience of the place to every part of Europe. It's no great trip from here to Paris or London or Rome."

Thomas Wilson is a young English architect who decided to move his life and his career to the charming setting of Provence some years ago. He had studied civil engineering at Cambridge and had worked for six years in England in the construction business before deciding to start on his own as an architect. It so happened that his father, Peter Wilson, chairman of Sotheby's auction gallery, had owned an extensive estate in the neighborhood of Grasse since the end of World War II. The elder Wilson gave his two sons houses on the estate, and for Thomas Wilson the timing was exactly right.

It took the best part of a year for him to renovate the farmhouse. During that time the vision of what he wanted was very clear in his mind, and above all he wished to restore the charming and antique quality of an old Provençal farmhouse—a place that had fallen into neglect and had lost much of its original flavor. To this end he essentially gutted the interiors: moving an entire staircase; putting in fireplaces; and designing doors and windows consistent with the original house.

"This sort of thing is really very typical of my general approach to architecture of all kinds," explains Mr. Wilson. "I like to use local old materials whenever possible. They add depth and richness, not to mention the desired authenticity. I also think my work is more concerned with structural changes than with interior décor as such. I always find it interesting and rewarding to compare the before and after of any old house I redo. In an old house like this it's so much easier to appreciate the changes, and they're rather more dramatic than the ones I find when dealing with something newer. I can't say there has been any one particular influence on my work, but I've been much interested both in the classical work of Palladio and in contemporary Americans like Philip Johnson."

Work on his farmhouse near Grasse was basically a combination of restoration and original architecture—the original architecture, of course, retaining as many of the elements of the past as possible. Built of stone and mortar, and covered with rough render, the farmhouse retains the now fading reddish pink color it was painted in the 1930s. The color seemed right to Mr. Wilson, and he has been careful to retain the same feeling of rustic simplicity in the interiors. Natural materials have been used extensively, and furniture was chosen for comfort rather than for luxury. It has an authentic peasant look of centuries gone by.

"Over the years I brought much of the furniture down here," explains the architect. "I picked it up here and there, in many different places. If furniture is handsome and appealing, I think it will look fine wherever it is. But I've made no particular effort to 'decorate' in any sense of the word. And certainly there aren't any decorating trends here in Grasse. Serious interior design just became fashionable in this area a year or so ago, and now there are some French interior designers with shops in Cannes. No doubt there will be a good many changes in the future. But I do hope they will be careful to respect the materials they are working with and to understand the history and the setting. The good ones will, of course."

In any event, Mr. Wilson is careful to emphasize that he is an architect, not an interior designer. Since his architectural work is most often in the traditional manner, he finds contemporary design a most interesting challenge. "I really have to admit," he concedes, "that it's far easier to build a traditional house. There are so many models to consider, so many ideas that have already been explored, so many problems that have been solved. But I will say that contemporary architecture, with its simplicity and functionalism, is extremely rewarding when it comes out well."

For his personal life, however, it is more than apparent that he prefers another kind of simplicity—the simplicity of the past, found most convincingly in the enchanting Provençal farmhouse he has so carefully and lovingly restored. In a curious way, by simplifying his life to conform to a somewhat rustic mold, Thomas Wilson has succeeded in making his existence far richer and more ample. He finds it easy to give dinner parties for ten at least twice a week, and there are three guest rooms in the farmhouse always ready for the many friends and clients who stop over on their way through France. The house is irresistible, and there is about it an air of graciousness and peace that puts people at ease.

It is a graciousness and ease quite as evident in his approach to architecture, and it is no wonder that he has found a splendid career in this enchanted part of rural France.

Fields of flowers, olive groves, walled terraces and a view of the Alps create an idyllic setting for English architect Thomas Wilson's 300-year-old Provençal farmhouse. Roseate and rough-textured, it is built of stone and mortar covered with render.

A wooden door leads into the separate building,
once a stable, that now houses the dining room and
kitchen. The wide stripe painted around the
doorway (and around the shuttered windows)
serves as a visual accent—a rustic substitute for
architectural detailing.

OPPOSITE: *Highlights of the Living Room include the floor Mr. Wilson designed of Angers slate outlined in oak, and a mid-17th-century Lambeth tapestry. A tapestry-covered armchair and a weathered table, both Provençal, lend authenticity to the farmhouse restoration.*

LEFT: *The Dining Room features a refurbished, but original, beamed ceiling and a pair of fireplaces added during the year-long restoration process. At that time, too, the walls were covered with render and were incised in a diamond pattern with a homemade cogwheel.*

OPPOSITE: *A 17th-century carved and gilded mirror from Aix-en-Provence embellishes an otherwise simple fireside conversation area in the Living Room. Composed of two generous sofas and a small Provençal wooden table, the grouping reflects the architect's preference for comfort rather than luxury. Arrangements of dried flowers and grasses add muted color to the room's earthy tonalities.*

TAILORING A LONDON TOWNHOUSE

There is something a little out of the ordinary in finding an American interior designer so completely attuned to the English way of life as Billy McCarty. The fact merely emphasizes that a good designer can, and should, be at home in any period and in any style. But along with the requisite amount of talent and skill and ingenuity necessary for his profession, Mr. McCarty has achieved the special status of being an international designer in the literal sense of the word. He has brought into play all facets of his experience that include a career and a life that have been divided between the United States, France and England.

Arriving in London in 1963 to work for David Hicks, he soon won awards—among them the Burlington—for furniture and wallpaper designs. And now he has his own firm devoted to interior design. Nothing happens overnight, however, and he served a long apprenticeship in many areas of design. Among other pursuits, he studied architecture under Louis Kahn at the University of Pennsylvania, worked as a city planner in Philadelphia and was a draftsman for a New York City firm.

In creating the décor of this six-story 1830s London townhouse, Billy McCarty has paid homage to the best in English tradition and has respected all the significant elements of the English past. Yet, as always, he has injected into the design his own fresh and highly personal style. While the décor is entirely English in concept and feeling, it is more than likely that its being so undeniably English has much to do with Billy McCarty's American background. Often, of course, it is easier to see things at a distance and with the addition of another perspective. The McCarty design is no slavish imitation of an alien tradition but rather an interpretation of it in the designer's own terms.

In approaching this London townhouse, his own early experience studying architecture has been of enormous help. The fact can be discerned almost immediately from the imposing front doors, inlaid with mahogany and ebony, that he designed himself. The entrance hall beyond is entirely filled with an oversized coco-fiber mat, a favorite touch of his. The designer uses the mat not only because it is attractive but also because it helps protect the custom-designed carpets in other parts of the house. The overall feeling of the townhouse is one of enormous warmth and comfort—all elegance aside for the moment—with a red-lacquered Korean chest in the stairway hall setting the tone immediately. The designer's meticulous attention to detail can be seen in the same location, where wallcoverings and draperies are made of men's wide-wale corduroy suiting, with a special fourteen-inch wool fringe.

It is interesting, however, that none of his designs really resemble one another—except in the matter of extreme attention to detail. He spends endless time with fringes, hardware, rugs and even curtain rods, details that many a designer might well hurry by. For example, in the present décor he specified open papyrus blossoms for the curtain rod finials in the library. When the space was found to be too small to accommodate them, he took time to design closed papyrus buds instead. And he will think of other details, too, that tend to make his work unique and easily identifiable. The house stands on the corner of a lovely London square, and he made certain that all draperies were carefully lined to present a uniform view from the outside: yellow chintz for the front of the house and beige facing the side street. This sense of balance is characteristic of Billy McCarty's work.

"As much as possible I prefer to use favorite objects and furnishings that the client already owns," he says. "I think it's my responsibility to work with such things and to make any additions harmonize with them. Naturally, the idea is to do what is most appropriate and effective. For this house most of the antiques I added were acquired by the owner and me. She'd find things, and then I would find others. There was really no confusion, since we had long ago agreed about the goals we had in mind. It was a glorious treasure hunt."

Nevertheless, many of the objects and furnishings in the house did take a long while to find, largely because both owner and designer had definite ideas about what was needed. For instance, a large tapestry had originally been envisioned by them for the drawing room. The proper one was difficult to find, and then one day Billy McCarty happened upon a large and appealing eighteenth-century painting, a family portrait by Thomas Beach, a pupil of Sir Joshua Reynolds, who worked primarily in Bath. Once hung, the picture was an instant success, adding a great deal of panache and elegance. It is, both owner and designer agree, far more effective than a tapestry would have been.

Panache and elegance, in fact, are the first impressions made by any McCarty design. But he is careful to provide a gracious and relaxed kind of elegance that allows for great flexibility both in living and entertaining. Every eventuality is considered and provided for—from giving a formal dinner party to curling up on a comfortable sofa for a cup of tea and the morning newspaper. Producing an overall feeling of space and tranquility is another of the designer's goals, and it is eminently apparent in this London townhouse. Enormous sofas give a sense of stability, while movable chairs and stools provide necessary flexibility. For the designer it is a question of the careful combination of formality and informality. His use of color, too, is of great importance. He is comfortable with all ranges of the spectrum but believes that a London townhouse requires a unique palette. The generally gray light of the city, he feels, demands a certain richness and depth of color, and he used a lush palette indeed—ranging from deep muted greens and blues to indigos and violets in smoky velvet, with accents of rich eighteenth-century yellow damask.

"There are no elaborate rules in my profession," says Mr. McCarty. "You do the best you can, that's all. But I do have a number of what you might call idiosyncracies. Indeed, they might even be considered neuroses! I pay a great deal of attention to small details: the quality of a particular finish, the way a room is painted, the fringe of a drapery. Work that is badly detailed does not hold up, and a traditional and lovely English house like this one should be made to last. Isn't that the whole point?"

OPPOSITE: *On a refreshingly bright London day, the sun bathes a corner of the Drawing Room in a townhouse near Kensington Gardens with interiors by Billy McCarty. Light streams across the Thomas Beach painting,* Lady Sefton and Family, *and the Bechstein grand piano.*

RIGHT: *A handsome Louis XVI marble mantel was installed in the Drawing Room, along with late-17th-century English andirons. The elaborate gilt-framed mirror and the chair covered in 18th-century French damask are George II.* BELOW RIGHT: *An Indonesian carved figure and other antiquities—a small sculptured stone head, Persian ceramics and silver—displayed on a 19th-century Dutch parquetry commode in the Drawing Room add to the blend of soft, rich patinas.*

Warm muted colors and naturalistic motifs enliven the pair of Louis XIV chairs upholstered in contemporary needlepoint. The carefully chosen arrangement includes a blending of smoky tones for the Drawing Room walls, a taffeta-draped table and an 18th-century painted leather screen.

214

Mr. McCarty drew upon his training in architecture when he conceived the design of the octagonally shaped, bleached oak-paneled Library. A Ming stone war god surveys the scene from atop a Chippendale mahogany table. The velvet sofa fabric blends with other soft tones in the room.

LEFT: *In the Hall, 19th-century wrought-iron stairway balusters lead toward a 19th-century Korean lacquered cabinet topped by a pair of large Imari plates. Corduroy-covered walls provide both a warm, textured background and a neutral-toned foil for the door, cornices and moldings, which are painted in contrasting tones of graphite and terra-cotta—a design element favored by Billy McCarty.* OPPOSITE: *Two Pembroke tables flank the tailored baldachin above the bed in the Master Bedroom; a subtle print fabric used for the undercanopy, upholstered headboard and bedcovering lightens the look.*

A ROME DESIGNER'S SEPARATE SOLUTIONS FOR TOWN AND COUNTRY

In these days, when anyone who can lay claim to having more than one string to his lute runs the risk of being hailed as a "Renaissance man," the term might appear to be a dubious compliment. But there is no other that more aptly describes the versatility of Italian designer Giulio Coltellacci.

In one context he assumes the guise of creator of stage sets and costumes for the ballet, while in another he functions as a painter, a collector and an interior designer. In the field of the visual arts he is, and has been for years, a major force in the cultural life of Italy. As an interior designer Signor Coltellacci is not one of those who harps on a single theme. Far from it. Working as he does in various media, he is accustomed to letting his imagination take flight. A case in point is the way he has approached the decoration of two quite different residences, both his own.

His apartment in Rome, while apparently owing its great chic to the adroit manipulation of color, texture and form, is really indebted to the triumph of technique over limited space. His country house, on the other hand—casual, comfortable, conceding nothing to fashion—is precisely what it seems. It is an old house, well proportioned, one that has been left in its natural state. The house is valued largely for what it offers the owner: a tranquil refuge from city life and its many pressures. The contrast between what the designer has created for himself in these two entirely different contexts is simply a reaffirmation of the extraordinary versatility that serves as his artistic hallmark.

When in Rome, Signor Coltellacci lives and works in the *Palazzo Tittoni,* a labyrinthine Baroque-style complex built in the mid-nineteenth century. Later it was divided into apartments, but since none afforded a sufficiently large area for both living quarters and a studio, the designer chose to occupy two separate settings.

For living quarters he selected an area measuring just over two hundred and fifty square feet, plus a terrace—indeed a small space to arrange effectively. In drawing up the plans for it, he resorted to every magician's trick at his command to minimize the spatial limitations of the apartment. He widened the narrow living room by covering one entire wall with mirrors, and he lengthened it by providing another wall of transparent glass that opens to the small terrace. To further the illusion of space he was most careful in the use of pattern, largely restricted to a carpet that is a variation on the classical Roman stripe. And everything else—walls, ceilings, furniture coverings—is in various shades of pale beige. Even the original ceiling was lowered to give the room the illusion of greater width. The effect is far from stark, however, as Signor Coltellacci has filled the interior with green plants, and his own paintings adorn the remaining wall space. Since there is no space at all for a dining room, he designed an L-shaped counter that is half in the living room and half in the corridor. Concealed behind it is a small and compact kitchen.

Every part of the small apartment is put to excellent use. The entrance hall, for example, displays the designer's collection of molded glass. He especially prizes two vases—one by Gallé and another by Moser, both of whom worked at the turn of the century. It is no surprise that the bedroom, too, is small, and its arrangement represents another triumph of mind over matter. By relegating clothes closets and storage space to an adjoining dressing room and by recessing the bed into a mirrored alcove, the designer has achieved much additional space—both literally and figuratively. By making everything white, from wool carpeting to walls and woodwork, he has given the space a marvelous feeling of luminosity. A sofa, a worktable and bookshelves are the only furnishings. The room is simple, and one of his paintings hangs over the fireplace, serving as a kind of signature.

The studio is quite the antithesis of this small apartment. Originally the winter garden of the palazzo, it is a vast room enclosed on three sides by glass. The domed ceiling is thirty feet high at the center, and the floor is a handsome mosaic of geometric designs worked in multicolored marbles. Everything else is white. The one wall not given over to glass is filled with bookshelves and a fireplace that are surmounted by a balcony containing more books. The furniture here has been conceived on a large scale in order that nothing be lost in the generous space. Giant indoor trees furnish the décor, and working props include a nine-foot-long desk, a drawing board and a painter's easel—a designer's dream come true.

Impressive as the studio is, Giulio Coltellacci's great enthusiasm is *San Simeone,* his country house. Named for the saint whose tiny chapel stands on its grounds, it was built in the fifteenth century and rebuilt in the seventeenth. It originally belonged to a fabulous Medieval castle in the nearby village of San Gregorio. The designer came upon it one day quite by accident, while driving in the hills near Tivoli. What first caught his attention was the color of the house—red from the autumnal hue of the vine leaves covering it. In the spring, of course, the leaves are green and luxuriant. The setting delighted him, and the vista is enchanting. The house is perched atop a knoll overlooking a little valley, the whole surrounded by undulating hills. "And there are olive trees everywhere you look," says the designer proudly. It was love at first sight.

Once he had acquired the property, however, there was a certain amount of work to be done. But the designer was in no hurry to change the character of the house. "I made only the necessary alterations," he comments, "and otherwise left the place almost exactly as it was." A bathroom was installed, original flooring repaired, walls replastered, here and there an old beam strengthened or replaced. Nothing more was really needed, or wanted, and the décor now consists of rustic antiques, simple upholstered pieces and handwoven rugs from the Abruzzi mountains. There are some antique paintings, both portraits and landscapes, and not a single design trick has been used.

"E il mio paradiso!" says Giulio Coltellacci with a broad smile. And he really means it. This country house is surely his own particular corner of paradise. However, he cannot be entirely unhappy to return to his magnificent studio and apartment in Rome after a weekend in the country.

ROME APARTMENT

The challenge of a small apartment in Rome's Palazzo Tittoni excited designer Giulio Coltellacci's ingenuity. He maximized the sense of space in the Living Room by lowering the ceiling, filling one wall with mirror, another with sliding glass doors, and the floor with striped carpeting.

LEFT: *Defined by glistening dark-lacquered linear accents, the Entrance Hall is sparsely, but impeccably, appointed with a Japanese porcelain lamp, a Thai bronze hand and Art Nouveau vases by Moser and Gallé.*

BELOW: *The Living Room's neutral colors and grass cloth-covered walls and ceiling serve as an unobtrusive foil for contemporary art, including a stylized portrait by the designer. A grid of ceiling beams creates a geometric pattern that is repeated, on a reduced scale, by the trelliswork of a gazebolike terrace.*

An artist's dream come true, Signor Coltellacci's Studio was originally the winter garden of the labyrinthine Palazzo Tittoni. The space is glass-enclosed on three sides, with the fourth giving way to a fireplace, balcony and bookshelves. Vast and airy, the studio is topped by a skylighted dome that soars thirty-one feet high at the center. The floor, a geometric pattern of multicolored Italian marble, echoes the ceiling's iron gridwork. Thriving in this atmosphere of light, a jungle of potted plants winds its way upward on slender columns.

DESIGN STUDIO

COUNTRY VILLA

BELOW: *Scenic 19th-century wallpaper surrounds the upstairs Salon's antique stone fireplace.*
OPPOSITE: *The Kitchen's open hearth, original brick floor and beamed ceiling—conveniently supplemented by modern appliances—create an archetypal setting for country repasts.*

ABOVE: San Simeone, *the designer's country home, not far from Tivoli, becomes a colorful spectacle each autumn when the vines that completely blanket it turn a fiery red. Other seasons find it camouflaged in the colors of the surrounding hills.*

RIGHT: *Autumn vines frame a view of the Entrance Hall, with its pitched ceiling, rough masonry and brick floor. A large ceramic jar, produced locally, is a convenient receptacle for walking sticks and umbrellas.*

OPPOSITE: *Built in the 15th century and reconstructed two centuries later, San Simeone originally belonged to a Medieval castle in the nearby village of San Gregorio. Idyllically situated, it perches atop a knoll in a valley encircled by hills and studded with olive trees.*

RIGHT: *Simplicity of design characterizes the Master Bedroom, a restful haven decorated with a 19th-century canopied bronze campaign bed, an antique desk and a rug handwoven in the Abruzzi mountains. Ethereal accoutrements include a fragment of an antique angel and a delicate painting of Zephyr, the personification of the gentle west wind.*

THE PATINA

OF

OLD PARIS

As a rule residential neighborhoods begin to lose their cachet when more modern areas, better suited to current ways of life, are developed. Over the last ten years in Paris, however, the process seems to have been reversed. The sixteenth arrondissement, long considered the most elegant part of the city, has become noisy and crowded with expensive apartment buildings. Some of the more sensitive residents are making their way back to older neighborhoods—to the Faubourg Saint-Germain, the center of fashion for over two hundred years, and to the Marais, which has recently been invaded by a host of small shops and galleries.

The Marais, on the right bank of the Seine, was built for the most part in the seventeenth century and includes the Île Saint-Louis in the river itself. Many of its magnificent old houses, happily saved from demolition, have been turned into lovely apartments. In fact, even the simplest sort of house here has undergone astonishing modernization. There is no doubt that the Île Saint-Louis is the most exclusive section of the Marais and the first to have been restored extensively.

To live on the island is a rare privilege. Tall houses, dating from the age of the Sun King, Louis XIV, and set among lovely trees, are built around its shoreline. There are seventeenth-century houses on all sides, nobly proportioned buildings, many with historical tablets, wrought-iron balconies and high brick chimneys. Behind massive paneled doors studded with nails are inner courts where ancient paving stones and mounting blocks have remained the same since the days of the horse-drawn carriage. Little has changed since the time when Baudelaire and his friends gathered in the Hôtel de Lauzun to discuss poetry.

The rue Saint-Louis cuts lengthwise through the island and is crowded with small shops such as might be found in towns like Blois or Sarlat. But there are art galleries, too, and the best ice-cream maker in Paris. The atmosphere is provincial, and there is the feeling that everyone knows everyone else. Luncheon on the Île Saint-Louis is always a special treat for a Parisian—more so, if he or she is fortunate enough to be invited to the home of the Princess Claude Ruspoli. Cross the Pont Marie and walk toward her apartment. Push open the old gateway leading to the building in which she lives, and notice the courtyard paved with enormous antique stones. Her apartment is on the third floor, and no elevator disfigures the staircase.

Princess Ruspoli moved to the Île Saint-Louis long before it became the chic thing to do. She is one of those rare women who follows the dictates of fashion more for her own amusement than from any sense of obligation. From time to time her consistent good taste is suddenly "discovered" by those who follow the trends of the moment. Her great-grandfather was Charles Haas, a formidable man of the world and one of the tastemakers of his own generation. In fact, Marcel Proust used him as the basis of one of the most memorable characters in *The Remembrance of Things Past.* Princess Ruspoli has two sons who are descended on their father's side from the Marquis de Lafayette.

Despite the charm of her apartment, one is immediately drawn to the windows overlooking poplar trees and a view of the Seine. In the distance are the rooftops of the Marais, the dome of Saint Paul and the turrets of the Hôtel de Sens.

After this splendid view, the eye is drawn to the blazing fire in the living room. It burns in a handsome Louis XVI fireplace and emphasizes the antique rose and lemon tones of the room. Forming a group around the fireplace are chairs of many different shapes and styles, as much at home as the guests themselves, no matter what their origins. There are several Late Victorian armchairs covered with flowered velvet in the Rothschild manner, then a *causeuse* and some upholstered banquettes under the windows. Lighting comes from Second Empire lamps with rose-colored globes and from a pair of vitrines, one containing coral and the other rare stones. Scattered on small tables are objects that attract and reflect the light: tortoiseshell and marble, for example. At the back of the room the surfaces of a large tortoiseshell chest gleam like embers in a darkened hearth.

Princess Ruspoli travels extensively in Europe and the Far East. But perhaps the most enjoyable trips she takes are the excursions she makes in Paris itself. Shopping for her apartment is always a great adventure, and it takes her to many parts of the city in search of appropriate objects. She is fond of visiting antiques shops and most especially the Flea Market. She often returns from such expeditions weighed down with antique fabrics: heavy damask draperies, embroidered silk, cut velvet, elaborate tassels—all the treasures of Victorian opulence. In addition to fabrics, one of her great enthusiasms is wood paneling, and she has collected many charming examples for her apartment. There is Louis XVI boiserie in the salon, Louis XV in the small library and Empire in the entrance hall. All of it is extremely simple, from the country; however, there is nothing coarse or rustic about it.

The atmosphere of the apartment is undeniably French and is reminiscent of some ancient château—once famous, now showing its age a bit, but always charming. To this atmosphere the princess has added many Oriental touches from her travels to the Far East: seashells, lacquered boxes, porcelain cups. Paintings are of two kinds: those done by friends such as Geneviève Hase, who is one of the most notable French abstract painters, and seventeenth-century paintings quite as decorative as tapestries. She also has a passion for primitive paintings and painstaking landscapes that might be the Sunday work of some favorite uncle, avid sportsman and amateur painter. One of the rare charms of Princess Ruspoli's apartment is that everything in it suggests a novel or tells a story. Perhaps this is to be expected. The Île Saint-Louis, cut off from the rest of the world by the Seine, is surely a capital of romance.

Undoubtedly there are more luxurious apartments on the island, some more precisely in the style of Louis XIV, others in the latest contemporary design. But there is none that can claim an atmosphere more appropriate to this haven of enchantment, this island far removed from the noise, the crowds, the tediousness of reality.

An eclectic array of antique boiserie shapes the
lively architectural environment of Princess Claude
Ruspoli's Paris apartment on the Île Saint-Louis.
In the Entrance Hall, an Empire vitrine and pair
of pilasters add vertical accents and establish a
suitably ornate backdrop for Louis XVI consoles
and a medley of objets d'art. A floral still life,
placed in the deep well of a skylight, effectively
heightens the small room.

A blazing fire, elements of Louis XVI boiserie, antique musical instruments and a vitrine filled with seashells and minerals enhance the warm, personalized Salon. Leather and cut velvet upholsteries and rich draperies reflect the princess's penchant for antique fabrics.

In anticipation of a festive dinner party, the Dining Room's long refectory table is covered with Indian silk and set with glistening stemware and Chinese Export porcelain. Still life paintings and primitive landscapes lend quiet charm to the traditional atmosphere.

Matching leather-covered chesterfields and a low game table are grouped near the fireplace in the cozy Library. Converted 19th-century oil lamps illuminate walls lined with bookshelves, small landscapes and a modern still life from the Orient.

An airy delicacy infuses the princess's sky-hued
Bedroom, whose walls are papered with
Neo-Classically inspired panels. Bird and flower
imagery embellishes the chintz-covered Louis XVI
daybed and Louis XV chair, harmonizing with
several floral-patterned rugs.

*Latticework and Empire iron balcony railings
texture the façade of the* garçonnière *set in a
courtyard distinguished by age-worn paving stones.
Luxuriant trailing ivy mingles with bamboo trees,
potted plants and other greenery to create a
charming, gardenlike Parisian hideaway.*

AN ENCHANTED ENGLISH GARDEN

Among the most respected contemporary interior designers in Europe, the late John Fowler was perhaps the doyen. For over thirty years he showed owners how to restore, refurbish and make the most of their châteaux and rolling acres.

They came to John Fowler because he was unrivaled in the art of casual elegance. He could harmonize the thrust of a grand, and often architecturally awesome, house with the desire of its owners to live in a comfortable home. The total look was never showy, but the knowing eye can always recognize a Fowler room—with its painted furniture, misty colors and romantic flowered chintzes—at first glance. A handsome budget was often needed to achieve this deceptively simple look. For Mr. Fowler's legendary fame as a designer was equaled by his reputation for achieving results without sparing any expense.

In private life he hated to count the cost, and he was known as a magnanimous friend and a splendid host. "I love to give people a good time," he once admitted. "I'm wildly extravagant."

Homes that bear witness to the Fowler touch include some belonging to members of the British Royal Family, Baron Philippe de Rothschild, the Paul Mellons and the Astors. His last major assignment found him working on *Chevening*, the future residence of HRH the Prince of Wales. Sometimes, indeed, John Fowler found himself designing for the grandchildren of his first clients.

In recent years, although no longer taking an active part in Colefax & Fowler, the firm created in the 1930s by Lady Colefax, John Fowler led a closely scheduled life as adviser on interior decoration to the National Trust. Dovetailed between such assignments, there was his own private work. The latter ranged from the landscaping of a park to the interior design for a university library. He relished making plans he might not live to see completed, commenting, "I simply adore designing for posterity." He had a passionate belief in the future.

One plan, designed in his mind's eye and now in full bloom, was his country house, a cottage *orné* from which he commuted to London during the week and that was filled with friends on weekends.

"This house reflects what I do for other people, only on a diminutive scale," Mr. Fowler explained. "Frankly, it looks humble enough to me. But when I come back from a day at, let us say, Blenheim Palace, I find nothing jars. What I wanted here was something utterly unpretentious, very comfortable, with a certain elegance and informality—and the feeling that you can sit down anywhere without even having to move a chair."

As might be expected, everything in the house and its gardens harmonizes astonishingly well. So, too, did the owner: John Fowler, a distinguished-looking gentleman quite in rapport with his surroundings, dressed in a tattersall shirt and vintage cream-colored corduroys of great panache.

Relaxing after an early Sunday morning foray into the garden with trug and sécateurs, he talked about his house and the ideas that went into it. Essentially he saw the house as a distillation of his favorite themes and hallmarks, reflecting his attitude toward life: a feeling for warmth and intimacy, a desire for comfort, the use of design that is classical without being rigid. He showed his delight in eighteenth-century decoration, but he used it realistically and avoided anything that might suggest uncompromising perfection.

John Fowler loved pleasant surprises. In the garden, for example, a sudden turn might reveal an eighteenth-century garden seat in a vine-covered secret place. He had a passion for growing things as well, and he made sure that at all seasons the interior of the house and the garden itself were bound together. On every lattice window there were fronds and branches of greenery. Ivies, honeysuckle, clematis and roses rampaged over and around the outside of the house, and inside were bowls of flowers and nature prints. Flowers lend their shape to candleholders and wallpaper prints.

The history of the house complemented the late owner's love of make-believe. It was constructed in the 1730s by the St. John family on the site of a building reputed to have been constructed for the meeting of Catherine of Aragón with her future husband, Prince Arthur, elder brother of Henry VIII. It was called *King John's Hunting Lodge.*

"It was used as a *rendezvous de chasse,* a place where the hunt could meet before the riders set off," explained John Fowler. "But I call it *The Hunting Lodge,* because it sounds less pretentious."

He bought the house in 1947, and it was in a state of near ruin. During the postwar period the law stated that only a small sum could be spent on structural repairs. Undaunted, the designer simply saw this restriction as another challenge.

"When I first arrived," he reflected, "there was deep snow—and a few moldy cabbages. I had to wait a year before I could get a license to spend more than £800. Then, of course, I had to sell my harpsichord to pay for the road!"

Since then, the house has been enlarged, and the two acres of gardens look as if they had been established for generations. With the English countryside all around him, John Fowler felt contented in his enchanted gardens. He was there on one of those strange leaden days devoid of sun when all the colors become muted. Raindrops hung from the early morning cobwebs lacing together the tendrils of a clematis. It was a peculiarly English day. The creeper on the summerhouse roof had just been pruned, and a collection of holes had been revealed—the ravages of inquisitive squirrels and woodpeckers. Despite having to patch up their destruction, John Fowler found great companionship with the local wildlife. "Blue jays, magpies and green woodpeckers," he related. "All the most decorative birds!" In the summer the garden room is flooded with sunlight and birdsong.

What feeling did he get from his country house and the lovely gardens surrounding it? Perhaps not peace exactly, John Fowler suggested, for that comes from communicating with the soul.

"I'm an incurable romantic at heart," he observed, "although I do try to stifle it. Romantics usually get hurt. But I do have this very English love of seeing things grow. I derive great pleasure from the sense of order I find in the way my garden grows—and an infinite feeling of calm."

BELOW RIGHT: *A grassy path leads past an 18th-century-style gate to designer John Fowler's cottage* orné *tucked away in England's Hampshire countryside. Original stone urns surmount the gabled Gothic Revival façade of the residence. Clipped and formalized trees and hedges are planted alongside flowering borders and backdropped by informal woods.* DETAIL: *A casual arrangement of garden flowers rests on an 18th-century garden seat.* OPPOSITE: *A pineapple finial, a symbol of welcome, adorns the Gothic-spirited Summer House.*

The formal garden thrives within the romantic natural environment of woods and water. Hornbeam hedges define the path from a small lake; strict rows of Portuguese laurel are clipped to form garden walls and rounded to resemble orange trees—as in a French or Italian garden.

Mr. Fowler's interpretation of the 18th-century style, as evidenced in the Sitting Room, departs from the rigid classical approach. An informally balanced arrangement of comfortable furnishings achieves his deceptively simple look of elegant ease. The Neo-Classically inspired serpentine-front satinwood commode, topped with enamel candlesticks and porcelain service plates, is set off by painted velvet bellpulls and a family portrait. A floral chintz and other soft-hued upholstery fabrics exemplify Mr. Fowler's dictum: "Never put a lot of bright colors together in a small room."

ABOVE LEFT: *Tulip-shaped tôle candleholders rise from a centerpiece of garden flowers on the Biedermeier maple Dining Room table.* ABOVE: *Seventeenth-century botanical prints flank a chinoiserie-decorated pierced wood basket resting on an 18th-century gilt bracket.* LEFT: *The front door opens into a small sunny Entrance Hall. A decorated antique serpentine pelmet borders rich dressmaker-detailed draperies that are a Fowler hallmark. A 17th-century plaque of the Emperor Tiberius hangs above the marble-topped Louis XVI painted console.*

John Fowler added the Garden Room, built of
rustic clapboard trimmed in white and roofed with
18th-century tiles, as a focal point for the garden.
Culinary herbs—winter savory, tarragon,
marjoram—and pyramids of clipped box trees grow
within dwarf-hedged borders.

An 18th-century French carved wood poodle gazes
out at the garden from his post beside a potted bay
tree in the sun-warmed Garden Room, where
bookcases house the noted designer's collection of
works on decoration. Coco matting covers the
scrubbed pine flooring.

ON THE ILE ST-LOUIS

He lives in a historical monument on the Île Saint-Louis overlooking the Seine; counts among his clients Guy de Rothschild and Antenor Patiño; pursues the glamorous life of *Tout Paris* with his attractive wife, Betty—and hates furniture.

François Catroux arrived on the Paris scene in the middle of the 1960s, when he settled there after ten years of constant traveling. One day a friend dropped in with an Italian lady. As they left, she asked if he would like to decorate her palace in Milan. The lady was couturière Mila Schön, and the project was an enormous success. Thus launched internationally, M. Catroux soon had projects all over the world—except in France.

"Most of the people I work for have their origins outside of France," he says. "I think it's a question of taste. Perhaps my designs don't seem 'decorated' enough to the French."

This fact hardly disturbs him, however, for he is delighted with his employers. "To talk about them would sound terribly snobbish, since they are all very well-known," he admits. Some of them come back to him many times.

"When people come to me," he concedes, "they either like what I do, or they don't. But when they do like it, they're 100 percent enthusiastic."

Such trust allows him to follow his own instincts rather than someone else's tastes. "My clients," M. Catroux observes, "already have a strong sense of what suits them and, more often than not, it corresponds with my own ideas." Most of the people he designs for become personal friends. He is especially pleased about the Hôtel Lambert, the seventeenth-century mansion belonging to Guy de Rothschild that is just around the corner from his own apartment. Together with an Italian designer he has redone the interiors to house the Rothschilds and their extraordinary collections of art, antiques and furniture.

"It was the challenge that appealed to me," says the designer. "The idea was to create a sort of museum that could be lived in with comfort. The building itself, of course, is a masterpiece."

His respect for architecture is not limited to

seventeenth-century Paris, however, and he is a great student of such architects as Neutra, Miës van der Rohe, Pei, Saarinen and Philip Johnson. Above all he admires their understanding of the simple line and their clean mastery of space. A native of Algeria, M. Catroux is also greatly influenced and intrigued by the opulent quality of Persian architecture. This influence is suggested in the rather stripped down, vaguely Oriental, look of his own apartment. He has lived here for some ten years now, changing the décor only twice. At first it was very contemporary—partly reflecting the era and partly because of precarious finances.

"I didn't have much money," he explains. "So I did most things in the least expensive way possible. Impressive for photographs, perhaps, but not so wonderful for living. Everyone adored plastic at the time, and on one level the old décor was quite a success. But finally we had enough of it."

Now everything is different, not only in his apartment but in his career as well. He recognizes that he has the reputation of being a very expensive decorator even in a very expensive city. He is not entirely sure why this is so, but he thinks it has to do with his insistence on quality.

"Coming to me is a little like going to Cartier," he says without false modesty. "I have everything made to order, and that does cost money."

His concern for quality is not exactly new. "Even in the beginning with this apartment," François Catroux points out, "when I was using inexpensive modern materials, I saw that all the basics were done in the best way possible. Only the superficial decoration was inexpensive." As a consequence the décor for his apartment can be arranged as conveniently as a stage set. "All the screens are mounted magnetically and can be lifted right off," he adds. "Nothing is nailed down. Certainly this isn't an inexpensive way of doing things. But if I decided to redo the place tomorrow in the style of Louis XIV, let us say, I could keep everything as it is until the last moment. Then it could all be dismantled in a day and be replaced immediately with Louis XIV. Et voilà!"

Although it is improbable that Louis XIV décor will replace bamboo screens and the leather and suede couches and pillows chez Catroux, the designer is quite capable of moving easily from the present to the eighteenth century and back again. As an illustration, he and his wife have a country house, an old Normandy manor, near Deauville.

"There's chintz everywhere," says M. Catroux. "But the house is Norman, so what can you do? It is important not to violate the essential mood."

His reputation for the mastery of contemporary design has a good deal to do with the fact that he is often confronted with old and crumbling interiors that need to be brought back to life. The contemporary approach seems to him the best solution. Yet when there are antiques available, he designs around them with great care.

"I don't throw everything out to make a contemporary setting," he adds. "That would be ridiculous. I love a mélange of old and new. But I do hate copies, and I will not produce something in faux Louis XVI—or faux anything else."

Perhaps his greatest ambition now is to be able to design an entire house, both interiors and exteriors. One of the problems, of course, is that such opportunities are rare in Europe today. "The fact is you have to let an architect work to the limits of his imagination, and there aren't many people who will allow that. For another thing, Europe is so full of lovely old houses. Why build something contemporary when you can have a beautiful antique house? I suspect the situation is rather different in the United States and in Latin America. And there are many exciting new designs in those areas."

Basically M. Catroux's approach to the new décor of his own apartment has been architectural. Even the furniture seems part of the architecture—elegantly unobtrusive and nearly nonexistent.

"I would never go out to buy two night tables for the bedroom," says the designer. "Never! It is space that interests me—masses that seem to melt together, the use of screens, different levels, different qualities of transparency. These are the effects I like. And I really detest furniture."

An Oriental atmosphere, at once natural and dramatic, infuses the Salon of designer François Catroux's Île Saint-Louis apartment. Pale areas are consistently set off by dark linear accents: bamboo wall panels are enclosed by black-lacquered wooden frames; platforms covered with coco matting rest on black-lacquered floors; and ceiling beams are complemented by dark, painted outlines. Within this predominantly light-colored and matte-textured environment, a stainless-steel chimneypiece adorned with a lacquered medallion, an Italian bronze Atlas and a pair of 18th-century Chinese covered jars contribute contrasting hard-surface luster.

Although he usually professes a disdain for furniture, M. Catroux has created a congenial atmosphere in the Salon with pairs of comfortable sofas and Miës stools surrounding a low table. An Indonesian water buffalo-shaped funeral urn and a gilded figure from Thailand add exotic mystery.

A movable baffle, made of the same bamboo screening that covers the walls, divides the Salon and filters the gentle Paris light. Before it, a large 17th-century Chinese lotus-shaped cloisonné bowl and two jardinières of flourishing orchid plants rest on a sleek contemporary console.

Multilevel platforms wrapped with Belgian wool fabric create textural interest and minimize the need for furniture in the simplified Master Bedroom. The highest level serves as a headboard, while lower ones provide ample surface areas for bedside accessories. Backdropping the tailored and natural-toned environment is the glistening panorama created by a 17th-century coromandel twelve-panel screen.

GREEK ISLAND

ODYSSEY

Some three and a half hours by sea from the ancient harbor of Piraeus lies the Greek island of Hydra. Rocky and almost treeless, with a principal town of barely three thousand in population and an area of eighteen square miles, it is small, isolated and peaceful. Once a fortified haven for pirates, Hydra dozes now under the southern sky, its handsome white buildings reflecting the Aegean sun. The pressures of the twentieth century are far removed, and unhurried island activities revolve around sponge fishing, the weaving of cotton and an occasional venture into shipbuilding.

Here, in this idyllic and primitive setting, Richard Tam and his associates, Oliver Pollard and Gary Craig, have created a most unusual house—a house at once contemporary and timeless, alien to the island and simultaneously an integral part of it. Mr. Tam is pleased to call his house a "space-age Atlantis," and the idea is an intriguing one.

The view and the setting enjoyed by the house almost succeed in making interior design superfluous. The house is situated on the steep slopes of the town, and below it the harbor of Hydra forms the stage of a vast amphitheater. The location is dramatic and unparalleled, one that the designer and his associates found irresistible. They saw the opportunity of creating a peaceful and beautiful way of life, contemporary and functional, yet quite in keeping with the ancient traditions of the island. It was an experience none of them wished to miss—an opportunity that might not come again.

In the beginning the house, apart from the view and its unique setting, offered little inspiration. Hardly more than a nineteenth-century ruin, it contained a series of small, dark rooms—a "lot of chopped-up space," as Richard Tam succinctly puts it. There was a great deal to be done. Most of the walls were taken down, for example, and master suites were arranged on different levels. A swimming pool, which took six months to complete, was carved out of solid rock. And endless time was required to complete the meticulous landscaping on the half-acre of land adjoining the house.

For what became a project of virtual reconstruction local artisans were used. This created a number of problems, however, since no one on the island had ever seen a house quite like it before. Most of the houses in Hydra were given over to pine furniture and naked light bulbs—with here and there an attempt at ostentation. Greek workmen were somewhat mystified by Richard Tam's sophisticated ideas, many of them not having even encountered such ordinary design accessories as the rheostat. Nevertheless, all the furniture in the house was made by island craftsmen or brought in from Athens by boat. Delays were common. The journey was complicated, but the goal was a simple one: to create an environment where everything would please the eye and function with ease.

In such worldly centers as London or Paris or New York—in Athens itself—Richard Tam's approach would hardly have been startling. In the context of the remote island on which his ideas came to life, however, it was. "Any space can serve any function" is possibly the major tenet of his design credo, an elegantly simple and flexible concept unknown to the people of Hydra. And until the house was completed, they did not understand what was being done. Perhaps not even then.

There is little revolutionary, however, about what Mr. Tam and his associates have created. It is true that from an insular point of view the results might seem unexpected and wildly out of the ordinary. But beauty and elegance do not lead to ostentation, and the renovated house is—above everything else—simple. There is nothing stiff or formal about it, and the end result, as the designer describes it, is "entirely comfortable."

Natural materials were used extensively. Stone and wood predominate, giving the house an unquestioned authority to belong exactly where it is. Even though the interiors may seem at first too sophisticated for their island setting, the house itself grows naturally from the rugged slopes of Hydra. In order to offset the restrictions of a small island, the designer manipulated the space with care, using high ceilings and French windows to extend the house in all directions. Nothing was done for the sake of drama but simply, as Richard Tam says, to make the house and its grounds "a beautiful experience in living."

Emphasis on the contemporary, on concepts of simplicity and comfort and flexibility, extends to the furniture and art and objects gathered in the house. With few exceptions there is nothing at hand either rare or antique or irreplaceable. Everything is to be used and enjoyed, to form part of a pleasant experience. There is no possible room for pretension. Decorations are attractive and informal: museum reproductions from Athens, a brass chandelier found in a junkyard, plants, colorful pillows. Out of preference art is the work of young, gifted and relatively unknown painters. Gary Craig, for example, produced many of the paintings in the house. In particular, there is a large and extraordinary one by him in the dining room, combining gold and silver leaf with gleaming boat lacquer.

"It's not what something costs that's important," says Richard Tam. "It is how well it succeeds in making one's life richer."

For this reason the décor of the house focuses largely on the contemporary world of art and design. Against all odds the results are magical.

"When people begin to concentrate exclusively on the past," says the designer, "there will be no tradition of modern art, nor of interior design."

So the house contains little of what might be expected on an island with roots in the classical past. There are few indications of the glory that was Greece. Indeed, a polyurethane column from Italy casually displayed certainly suggests the unimportance of history in terms of contemporary living. But the irony of such design comments is delicate.

These touches in no way diminish Richard Tam's respect or enthusiasm for the past. He and his associates have in fact made a conscious effort to harmonize the contemporary idiom with the ancient world of Greece. Richard Tam has by no means turned his back on that world. But rather, like Janus, god of arches and doorways, he has fashioned a house that succeeds in looking in two directions at the same time.

Refurbishing a 19th-century hillside home on the Greek island of Hydra was an adventure designer Richard Tam and his associates could not resist. The stone Terrace—abloom with oleander and geraniums—overlooks a splendid view of town and harbor that justifies their efforts.

In the Entrance Hall, breezes circulate and sunshine filters through latticework doors and louvered shutters. Stone walls washed in terra-cotta and a glistening floor of native Volos stone reflect the designers' fondness for the colors and textures of rugged natural materials.

Understated color and simplified geometric forms
combine in the unpretentious, yet sophisticated,
Living Room. Gleaming against the muted
background are brass candlesticks, a classically
inspired bronze figure and contemporary works by
Gary Craig—a gold and silver unicorn and a
lacquered four-panel screen.

An elongated honeycomb motif defines the
sculptured fireplace designed and built for the
Living Room by a Czech craftsman. The rough
stone floor, dense flokati rugs, smooth lacquered
tables and colorful plump floor pillows create an
effective harmony of texture.

262

Consistent with the rest of the residence in its
subtle color scheme, the Master Bedroom reconciles
rustic, antique and contemporary elements.
Large-scale furnishings—an unexpected Victorian
pine armoire and a draped platform bed—convey a
sense of controlled clarity.

AN ENGLISH WEST COUNTRY PARSONAGE

"In architecture it is good manners to answer with your furnishings. I've done that here, with much pushing and pulling around, and I've fixed it the way I want—with Parson Kilvert and tradition breathing down my neck slightly."

Architect and interior designer David Vicary is speaking, as he climbs out of his gum boots and leads the way into his West Country parsonage. It is inevitable to wonder how the Reverend Francis Kilvert, the eighteenth-century diarist, would have felt about the décor arranged by the present owner. For it was here that the parson's thoughts on country life were set down in his *Diary*. The house is charged with nostalgia, both for Parson Kilvert's time remembered and for life in the grand manner, toward which David Vicary is predisposed.

And so—after viewing a hundred or more potential residences, none of which was appropriate architecturally, geographically or economically—he stumbled upon *Kilvert's Parsonage*, a romantic Georgian house veiled by a multitude of trees. Visitors now find their way to the parsonage with the help of a card printed in ecclesiastical Gothic and written with whimsy. "Keep hawkeyed for broken down 1825 Iron Gates in Hawthorne Hedge on RHS. Drive over fields, single Oak on left. Go on into wood," it reads.

The house was built by the Woods family who went on to build the town of Bath, and it is constructed in the characteristic gray and somber Bath stone. Inside, behind the heavily draped Irish-tweed curtain that skirts the front door, the atmosphere is completely Italian. In the enormous main hall the wainscot is simulated mahogany, and suspended from the ceiling is a Venetian chandelier, its candles half-spent and dripped wax hardened down their sides. Wall brackets hold more candles in careless disarray.

"It's my Miss Havisham touch," says Mr. Vicary, "though I don't go so far as cobwebs! Initially, the walls were clogged with distemper. I changed them from their traditional Bath biscuit color. And a good thing, too."

He describes the house as being "very grand

on a small scale." He is delighted with the original shell and with what he has achieved in the interior. "I have a passion for the country house thing," he comments, "and it's unbelievable what you can learn if you actually go at it."

It is not unusual to find David Vicary clad in a full-length paisley robe, scrambling eggs amid a clutter that would be untenable for more orderly individuals. Functional pots and pans are overlaid with ornaments, and food and furniture gather haphazardly in the Dutch-looking kitchen. Flake, the snow-white cat, prowls on the windowsill.

Maintenance of so many possessions does not worry their owner. "The navy," David Vicary explains, "taught me all about routine and scrubbing floors. Hard work doesn't worry me. A blitz, then I forget it. Anyway, I couldn't live in a plain and sparse room. Obvious, isn't it?"

The parsonage indeed suggests a counting-house with an untold wealth of clutter. But amid this keenly overstuffed home with another ten or more empty rooms still locked at the back, it is difficult to discover whether the owner finds his attitude toward the collections damning or admirable. There is a certain ambivalence. He is proud of his eye for detail, and you would have to be gimlet-eyed to wend your way through such a maze to find something as ordinary as, say, a mislaid bedroom slipper. Disorder hardly bothers him.

"What I need from my home is sympathy," he says, "and I get it. It meets my first requirements in a place to call my own: style, architecture and complete privacy. It's all here."

Upstairs the bedroom, known as The Kilvert Room—with its writing desk showing a diary in progress, and its four-poster—is much as it was in the days when the parson wrote here. The acacia tree mentioned in the diary can still be seen from one window, and another window has ivy festooned over the outside panes to form a filtered green screen. The room is charged with atmosphere. David Vicary surely developed his theatrical sense while working on sets for the ballet. The backdrop to this 1739 room includes a hip bath with a bottle of Sherry and biscuits alongside, prints of Stonehenge and portraits of prominent figures in the annals of English history.

The house itself assails the senses with color. The designer has an acute visual perception. Of this heightened awareness he says, "Colors pour in here very strongly in order to create the overall effect I want—an effect of a certain grandeur. After all, I was schooled to that mood." A relative is about to disgorge a load of Queen Anne mirrors and silver, so more rooms will have to be decorated to house these additional treasures.

David Vicary acquired considerable knowledge from the experience of working with the renowned interior designer John Fowler. And today his own assignments often combine work with London designer David Mlinaric.

People for whom he has done interiors include names to conjure with: Clore, Getty, Heinz. Previous projects have ranged from working for the queen mother, who questioned the practicality of kitchen floor matting, to assisting Mick Jagger.

"Usually I have twelve things going on at once," he says. "Paul Getty's library at Rossetti's house in Chelsea is a particularly interesting one."

Around the grounds of Kilvert's Parsonage are stables and other outbuildings. Over the stable door is a white horse head with a plant trailing across its mane. A dovecote by the kitchen is a model of Mr. Vicary's previous house. Beyond are signs of present endeavor in the garden: old-fashioned roses carefully mulched and growing among the ancient fruit trees, and apple trees with heavily laden autumn boughs.

David Vicary is presently prepared to do battle with the overgrown thicket. With his abrupt walk, his bushy hair, his slightly nervous and questioning manner of speech, he suggests Ratty in the classic tale *The Wind in the Willows,* and he appears quite in keeping with his grand but most private setting.

Surely there is no one who can sum up the true spirit of Kilvert's Parsonage better than David Vicary himself: "I love enigmas, mysteries and the calling back of what was yesteryear."

Located in Wiltshire's Vale of the Avon and surrounded by elms, grasslands and chalk downlands, Kilvert's Parsonage, a twenty-five-room Early Georgian house, was built from stone quarried at nearby Bath. Inscribed on the keystone above the front door is the date of construction: 1739. The Tuscan-style columned porch was added to the structure in 1760.

OPPOSITE: *Architect/designer David Vicary's feeling for history is reflected by the Victorian-style accumulation in the Red Room, which is named for its 1840 Brussels rug. Nineteenth-century cottons cover chairs and tables, and English bellpulls flank a 1690 portrait of Catherine of Braganza.*

ABOVE AND ABOVE RIGHT: *Antique fringe trims the festooned draperies framing a window-seat niche in the Red Room that overlooks the tree-lined garden. Old roses, a Derbyshire spar obelisk and tent-pole finials cluster on a painted table below a 1648 portrait of a dignified Vicary ancestor.*

OPPOSITE: *Mr. Vicary's passion for country houses is exemplified by his Dutch farmhouse-inspired Kitchen. Warm-toned stippled walls set off transfer-printed plates from an extensive Spode collection; other examples adorn a large oval dining table covered with a Portuguese cloth.*

Each corner of the country Kitchen offers a potpourri of treasures. RIGHT: *A still life on a window recess includes a Bath-stone corn sheaf, a French rabbit terrine, a Sicilian fish-shaped bottle for olive oil and a Minton chicken jelly mold.* BELOW RIGHT: *Two Spode plates depicting Alexander Pope's villa at Twickenham stand behind Leeds and Wedgwood creamware. A Yorkshire estate map is above the butcher's table.*

271

AMBIENCE

IN

NORTH AFRICA

"Throughout the night they shall prepare exquisite beverages and rest on fine carpets and beautiful cushions." Such is one of the more appealing descriptions of that paradise reserved for the sons of the prophet in the Koran. It applies as well, quite literally, to the small village of Hammamet in Tunisia, which has been enjoyed over the past forty years as a sophisticated holiday oasis for the initiated. Unspoiled, the village lies some thirty kilometers from the capital city of Tunis.

On the site of ancient Carthage, the capital is at the threshold of the western Mediterranean, bounded on the southeast by Libya, on the west by Algeria and on the north and east by the Mediterranean. Founded by the Phoenicians, Carthage under Augustus Caesar was one of the great cities of the Roman Empire, rich with imposing classical architecture. But the passing of the centuries saw the rise and fall of many a civilization along the North African coast. In the seventh century there was an Islamic conquest of Tunisia, various Berber dynasties took control from the twelfth to the fifteenth century, and the Turks arrived in the 1500s. By the late-nineteenth century Tunisia was a French protectorate, and it did not receive fully independent status until 1957.

As early as the twelfth century tiny Hammamet, on the gulf of the same name, was an important military headquarters. History, however, soon passed the village by, and it dozed peacefully under the North African sun for almost eight hundred years, a small seaside fishing community with a gentle climate and a profusion of fruit and palm trees. The houses were small, painted white and largely sealed against the sun, their design a traditional North African mixture of straight lines and gracefully undulating curves.

Then, in the late 1920s, a rather special company of invaders began to arrive from Paris. The Hungarian conductor George Sebastian, often called the "Pygmalion of Hammamet," was perhaps the first to have seen the possibilities of this small Tunisian village as a holiday resort of a most unusual and appealing kind. In 1928 he restored one of the larger houses for himself, a gleaming white mosquelike building with tall towers and a terrace overlooking the sea. Word spread to a select circle in Paris, and others soon followed in his footsteps—among them, writer André Gide and fashion designer Elsa Schiaparelli. Hammamet was, at that time, for the very few. The village was a small protected casbah pointing like a white finger into the North African Mediterranean.

Little by little the French continued to discover Hammamet, and other waves of stylish invaders came, including painters Henri Matisse and Paul Klee, the Baron Edmond de Rothschild, and fashion designer Hubert de Givenchy.

One of those lured to Hammamet in the 1960s was a French actor and singer who, like so many before him, was charmed by the magic of North Africa, its dramatic scenery and evocative history. He acquired a small, traditionally built and unprepossessing fisherman's house in the medina.

Acting as his own architect and interior designer, he expanded the small house, retaining all the ancient elements of the local architecture and at the same time adding every modern convenience. For the interiors he made a particular point of being faithful to the locale and avoiding the jarring notes of another culture. He made extensive use of Roman columns found in the neighborhood, and even the top of his dining room table is a mosaic excavated from neighboring Sousse.

Nevertheless, there is a feeling of the dramatic, too, and homage is paid to the exotic past of North Africa. The owner remodeled the interiors to suggest an almost Byzantine atmosphere, marked by the visual continuity of the columns and a stunning vaulted bedroom. In fact, the only boundaries between rooms are arches supported by antique columns. A terrace was added, and some of the rooms now extend directly over the Mediterranean.

He lives in a manner and in a setting that seem suited to the locale—although few of the native residents live in quite the same manner, much preferring to seal their houses against the sun. The feeling, however, is rather romantic and European.

He has done precisely what so many other Europeans have done: He has created a house that looks the way a house should look in Hammamet, at least to the European eye. The fact that this almost fictional décor is possible can be credited to a large extent to the flexibility of Islamic architecture. It is a form of design that is not in many ways logical but is based, rather, on tradition and a certain amount of intuition. It is extremely easy for Europeans to adapt their own ways of life to the existing context.

Today Hammamet is changing, and, of course, it is far better known than it was in the days when George Sebastian "discovered" it in 1928. From France there have come various waves of people with taste and imagination and unique vision. After World War II a rather more extensive invasion of Hammamet occurred. That period brought what are sometimes called the "new Romans": Italian designers, actors and art dealers. Peggy Guggenheim came as well, and tiny Hammamet was no longer a retreat for a few discerning Parisians. Warrens of houses in the casbah were dismantled, restored, redecorated. Souks were cleaned to welcome visitors from the new hotels lining the beach. Hammamet is a mosaic of North Africans, Italians, French, English and Americans.

For all the international invasions, however, Hammamet still retains its charm and traditional character—not only because of rigid government regulations about construction and the preservation of the past, but because of the nature of the foreigners drawn to Hammamet. They have been people of taste, like the owner of the present house—people who have made every attempt to preserve traditions, only redefining them slightly. They have done nothing to damage the mystique that attracted them to Hammamet in the first place. Basically, the village is still for the discriminating few, and the North African past and traditional Tunisian hospitality are very much in evidence.

"For those who come to know it," wrote Procopius, a sixth-century Byzantine historian long familiar with the area, "this is the most magnificent paradise." His opinion stands unchallenged today.

OPPOSITE: *A groin-vaulted terrace, added during the renovation of this Tunisian seaside villa overlooking the Gulf of Hammamet, is supported by sections of locally excavated Roman columns. The floor, modeled after a Byzantine mosaic, was reconstructed at the neighboring Sousse Museum.*

ABOVE: *An arched colonnade allows a flow of air from garden to terrace to a Living Room addition built directly over the Mediterranean Sea. Tunisian accessories—straw matting, cushions made of native Berber wool and a strapped and studded chest—complement the Islamic architecture.*

A procession of receding arches creates a sense of depth for a vaulted Sitting Area. Banquettes covered with batik-wrapped pillows and low dividing walls adorned with locally found objects fill the space between the span of arches. Indirect lighting is augmented by soft candlelight.

LEFT: *Built-in banquettes, softened by colorful pillows, line an alcove designed for dining. The mosaic tabletop is another reconstruction from nearby Sousse, and the vitrine houses an assortment of native shells. Sliding grilles help to control the clear seaside light.*

OPPOSITE: *A pool paved with marble, in the shape of a Byzantine baptistry, serves as a sunken bathtub in an area adjoining the Bedroom. Another reference to antiquity is the roughly textured supporting column. European strapped-leather chairs and iron candelabra add linear definition to the vaulted open space.*

Flaming torches dramatically illuminate the residence, once the home of a local fisherman. The antique supporting columns on the terrace, each with a unique texture, and the free-standing column in the garden imbue the romantic structure with a sense of Tunisia's classical past.

CREDITS

PHOTOGRAPHERS

L. Bartzioti *106-115, 126-137, 150-155*

Michael Boys *96-105, 156-163*

Demetri Bassoumis *256-263*

Robert Emmett Bright *36-41, 42-49, 138-149, 186-191, 192-201, 218-227, 274-283*

Allen Carter *64-75, 164-173*

Robert Fisher *58-63*

Pascal Hinous *18-27, 76-85, 174-185, 228-237, 248-255*

I. Ioannides *106-115, 126-137, 150-155*

Derry Moore *10-17, 28-35, 50-57, 238-247, 264-273*

Martin Pollard *116-125*

Tim Street-Porter *202-209*

Edward Woodman *210-217*

WRITERS

The following writers prepared the original *Architectural Digest* articles from which the material in this book has been adapted:

Susan Heller Anderson
Helen Barnes
Sam Burchell
Allen Carter
Adrian Cook
Elizabeth Dickson
Luis Escobar
Steffi Fields
Philippe Jullian
Rosemary Kent
Elizabeth Lambert
Keitha McClean
Ruth K. Miller
LaVerne Prager
Paige Rense
Suzanne Vidor

ACKNOWLEDGMENTS

Many staff members and associates of *Architectural Digest* magazine were instrumental in adapting the original elements and producing the new material which appears in INTERNATIONAL INTERIORS. We appreciate their efforts equally, and thank those who were most involved alphabetically:

EVERETT T. ALCAN, Vice President Operations, Knapp Communications Corporation.

ALICE BANDY, The Knapp Press, Manager/Administration.

ROSALIE BRUNO, Vice President Circulation, Knapp Communications Corporation.

SAM BURCHELL, *Architectural Digest* Senior Editor, who rewrote and adapted the original text.

RICHARD E. BYE, The Knapp Press, Managing Director.

ANTHONY P. IACONO, *Architectural Digest* Production Director.

JOANNE JAFFE, Caption Writer.

CLAUDIA KAPLAN, The Knapp Press, Associate Editor.

PHILIP KAPLAN, Vice President Graphics, Knapp Communications Corporation, who supervised all graphics.

BRUCE KORTEBEIN, Design Consultant.

JOHN LINCOLN, *Architectural Digest* Antiques Consultant.

JOYCE MADISON, Chief Copy Editor.

CHRISTOPHER PHILLIPS, *Architectural Digest* Associate Editor.

HENRY RATZ, Production Director.

MARGARET REDFIELD, *Architectural Digest* Copy Editor.

GAYLE MOSS ROSENBERG, *Architectural Digest* Captions Editor.

STUART H. SALSBURY, *Architectural Digest* Art Consultant.

JUDITH SAMUEL, Caption Writer.

MARK TRUGMAN, The Knapp Press, Promotion Manager.

ELLEN WINTERS, The Knapp Press, Administrative Assistant.

J. KELLEY YOUNGER, *Architectural Digest* Managing Editor.